Mounta Colorado Springs

A Guide to the Pikes Peak Region's Greatest Off-Road Bicycle Rides

SECOND EDITION

DAVID CROWELL

FALCON®

GUILFORD, CONNECTICUT
HELENA, MONTANA

AN IMPRINT OF THE GLOBE PEQUOT PRESS

Contents

The Rides

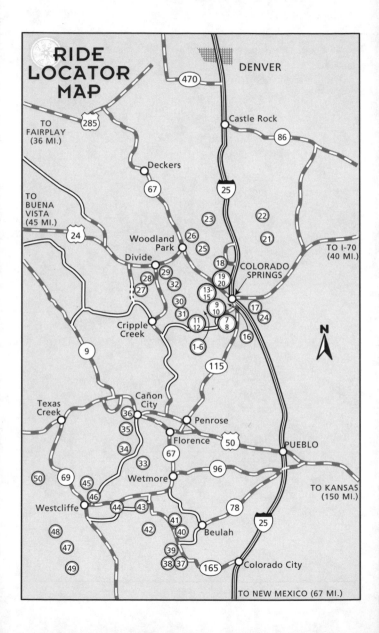

RIDE LOCATOR MAP

DENVER

470

TO FAIRPLAY (36 MI.)

Castle Rock

86

Deckers

67

25

TO BUENA VISTA (45 MI.)

24

Woodland Park

Divide

23

22

21

26

25

18

19
20

COLORADO SPRINGS

TO I-70 (40 MI.)

28 29

32

13-15

9
10

17

24

27

30

31

11
12

7
8

16

Cripple Creek

1-6

9

115

Texas Creek

Cañon City

36

Penrose

35

Florence

50

PUEBLO

34

67

33

96

50 69 45

Wetmore

TO KANSAS (150 MI.)

46

44 43

78

25

Westcliffe

41
40

Beulah

48

42

47

39

49

38 37

165

Colorado City

N

TO NEW MEXICO (67 MI.)

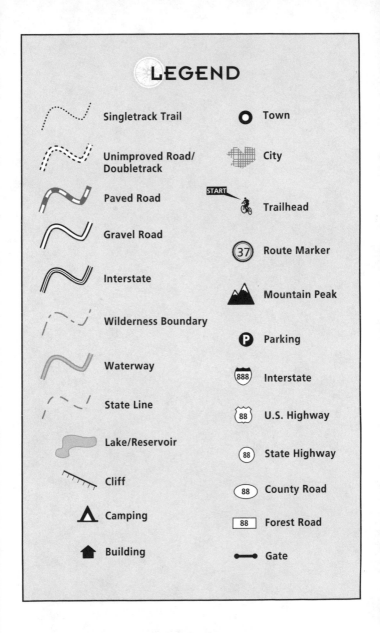

LEGEND

Symbol	Description	Symbol	Description
	Singletrack Trail	O	Town
	Unimproved Road/Doubletrack		City
	Paved Road	START 🚲	Trailhead
	Gravel Road	(37)	Route Marker
	Interstate	▲	Mountain Peak
	Wilderness Boundary	P	Parking
	Waterway	(888)	Interstate
	State Line	(88)	U.S. Highway
	Lake/Reservoir	(88)	State Highway
	Cliff	(88)	County Road
	Camping	88	Forest Road
	Building	•—•	Gate

Acknowledgments

My life has been touched by many people, all of whom helped make me who I am! A global thanks to all my friends . . . you are my strength. Thanks.

This newly updated edition owes its existence to many:

My editors, Scott Adams and Joan Wheal. Thanks for understanding quirky writers.

The production staff, for taking all this new info and making it look good.

Jaan and Jonell, for going above and beyond.

Rick Ellsworth of the U.S. Forest Service. You give me faith in our forests' future.

Tim Halfpop, Kip Biese, and Dave Guinn, for helping me find a starting point for this update.

Tim Watkins and Trina Lutwiniak, for keeping the biking spirit alive.

Eric Todd and Tony Orr, for keeping me humble.

Mother Earth, for everything.

Heidi, for making everything worthwhile.

And Dawson, for just being you.

Get Ready to Crank!

Mountain bikers, beginner to expert, all share a common need: A place to ride. *Mountain Biking: Colorado Springs* gives the fat-tire enthusiast the skinny on where to ride.

Now you can put variety into your mountain biking diet! The 50 rides in this book range from easy rollers to lung-busting loops. You will be able plan rides knowing what's in store. *Mountain Biking* guides rate each ride for two types of difficulty: the physical effort required to pedal the distance, and the level of *bike-handling skills* needed to stay upright and make it home in one piece. We call these aerobic level and technical difficulty (the ratings are explained on pages 4 and 5).

Our aim here is threefold: to help you choose a ride that's appropriate for your fitness and skill level; to make it easy to find the trailhead; and to help you complete the ride safely, without getting lost. Take care of these basics and fun is bound to break loose.

The Pikes Peak Region and Beyond

Mountain Biking: Colorado Springs covers a lot of ground. Sixty-five miles north and south by 60 miles east and west to be precise. That's 3,900 square miles! To make the guide easy to use, the rides have been grouped into five geographic sections: Colorado Springs, Woodland Park–Divide, Cañon City, San Isabel Lake, and Wet Mountain Valley–Sangre de Cristo Mountains.

The majority of the rides are within a thirty-minute drive of Colorado Springs, and the rest are reasonably close. Each section has special information pertaining to the area and additional rides that couldn't be packed in. A brief synopsis of the sections is in order.

The Colorado Springs area presents the core curriculum of rides with the main campus being Pikes Peak, North Cheyenne Canyon, and the area's extensive park system. These rides all lie within minutes of downtown Colorado Springs and run the full gamut of abilities.

Woodland Park–Divide rides put variety in the schedule. Most of the rides are rated moderate and the scenery is incredible. The crowds here will vary, but they tend to be smaller than in Colorado Springs.

If nearby solitude is what you want, Cañon City is the region. The crowds are few and the rides are moderate to strenuous. The Tanner-Stultz loop is one of the most technically challenging in this guide. As temperatures soar in the summer, trail conditions become dry and loose.

San Isabel Lake offers it all! The listed rides are for the hard-core. Moderate and easy rides can also be found in the region. The drive time of about two hours usually filters out casual riders. Great singletrack and challenging terrain are surrounded by unspoiled forest. Overnight camping is available as is some modest lodging. See the hand-built, medieval-style castle while in the region!

The Wet Mountain Valley is about a ninety-minute drive from Colorado Springs. Camping and modest lodging is readily available for weekend plans. The valley and the majestic Sangre de Cristo Mountains offer rides from easy to strenuous, good for all abilities. Lots of history here! Spanish conquistadores, German colonists, miners, and Ute Indians have all called this valley home. WARNING: Spending time here can be habit forming!

A Guide to the Guide

Most of the information in this book is self-explanatory. But if anything in a ride description doesn't seem to make sense, re-read the following explanation of our format.

Maps are clean, easy-to-use navigational tools. Closed trails are not usually shown on the maps but may be listed in the ride description. Each map has a symbol showing the north orientation. Make sure the map is properly oriented when you use it.

Elevation profiles provide a good look at what's in store by graphically showing altitude change, tread, and ratings (see page 7). Out-and-back rides are shown only in one direction. Simply reverse the direction of travel for the return profile.

The rest of the information is listed in an "at-a-glance" fashion. It is divided into twelve sections:

Ride number refers to where the ride falls in this guide. Use this number when cross-referencing between rides for an easy way to find the descriptions.

Ride name refers to the most common name for the trail. Many trails in the region have been changing names faster than they can make signs. Maps might still show the old names and numbers. This shouldn't be a problem—except maybe at the coffee shop.

Location tells, in general, where the ride is.

Distance gives the ride's length in miles.

Time is an *estimate* of how long it will take to complete the ride. It is trail time and does not include stops. If the ride is rated as more difficult or strenuous than what you usually ride, add some time to the estimate. If it's rated a lot higher, add a big chunk of time! It might take strong, skilled riders less time. Compare your ride times with those listed in the guide and adjust your estimates accordingly.

Tread describes what the tires ride on. Singletrack, dirt road, and doubletrack are common examples. A note or two will be included if conditions aren't good.

Aerobic level *estimates* the physical challenge of the ride. The levels are: easy, moderate, and strenuous. A note here will describe any special details pertaining to the rating.

Easy rides are mostly flat, but may include some rolling hills. Any climbs will be short.

Moderate rides will have climbs; some might be steep. Long, gradual hills also fall in this category. Strenuous sections may occur, but the majority of the ride is moderate. Even on a moderate ride, some steeper sections may force some cyclists to dismount and walk.

Strenuous rides put the granny gear to work! Not many people will ride these without walking. The steeps may be long, grueling tests of endurance, power, and determination.

These ratings are for comparison's sake. Easy rides can still have you gulping air and moderate ones may have you walking. Walking a bike is a perfectly legitimate way to transport it. Remember, this guide is for beginners to experts. Therefore, compare your first rides to the levels to get a feel for the classifications.

The aerobic levels are paired with ratings for **technical difficulty**. In this rating, a scale from 1 to 5 quantifies how much biking skill is needed to keep the rubber-side down. Here's a quick explanation of what the technical difficulty ratings mean:

Level 1: Basic bike-riding skills needed. The tread is smooth and without obstacles, ruts, or steeps.

Level 2: Mostly smooth tread with minor difficulties. Ruts, loose gravel, or obstacles may exist. However, they are easily avoidable.

Level 3: Irregular tread with some rough sections, steeps, obstacles, gravel, sharp turns, or open switchbacks. These will have route options or "lines" through them.

Level 4: Rough going! The tread is uneven with few smooth sections. The line is limited as it goes through rocks, roots, branches, ruts, sidehills, narrow tread, loose gravel, and switchbacks. These obstacles often occur on steeps!

Level 5: Continuously broken, rocky, root-strewn, or trenched tread with frequent, sudden, and severe changes in gradient. Slopes necessitating off-the-seat riding and nearly continuous obstacles exist. The line might be hard to find.

Pluses and minuses cover the in-between areas.

A ride's overall rating for technical difficulty describes the majority of the ride. Sections that rate higher can be found in the ride description and profile. Extreme obstacles may be listed along with the main rating or in the highlights section.

Again, these ratings are for comparison's sake. Riders proficient in gravel-riding techniques may have an easier time on one trail than riders who rip up the switchbacks. Gauge your ability on the first few rides against the scale to get a feel for the ratings.

Highlights is where to find the ride's emotional story. Qualities that make the ride unique and specific hazards will be listed here.

Land status describes ownership for each trail. The rides in this guide are mostly on public lands. Appendix B gives the information needed to contact the various land management agencies about rules, regulations, and updates.

Maps is a list of maps that show the ride's area. The USGS maps listed for the ride can be used for a more detailed view, and the Forest Service maps are useful in finding additional rides. They are interesting but might not show the ride's entire route. The topology markings on these maps show the climbs and descents, but so do the elevation profiles in this guide.

Access gives directions to the trailhead. The directions are from a common point in the region. Directions to that point may be found in each regional introduction. Access to the High Drive parking lot, which is the starting point for several rides in the Colorado Springs area, is detailed at the beginning of the Colorado Springs section.

The ride lists where to go and how to find your way back. Attached to the descriptions are odometer readings. These are *estimates!* Bike computers aren't the best measuring devices. But the readings should give a good idea of where things lie.

This guide doesn't pretend to be omniscient. Ratings are as accurate as possible. However, everyone is different. Individual riders seem to excel in different skills and this can affect the actual difficulty of a ride. A guide is a starting point. Every effort has been made to deliver an accurate account of the rides. Regulations, ownership, and even the land itself change. This guide should still get you home in one piece. If you have an inadvertent adventure, drop us a line.

Elevation Graphs

An elevation profile accompanies most ride descriptions. Here the ups and downs of the route are graphed on a grid of elevation (in feet above sea level) on the left and miles pedaled across the bottom. Route surface conditions (see map legend) and technical levels are shown on the graphs.

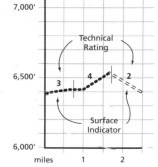

Note that these graphs are compressed to fit on the page. The actual slopes you will ride are not as steep as the lines drawn on the graphs (it just feels that way). Also, some extremely short dips and climbs are too small to show up on the graphs. All such abrupt changes in gradient are, however, mentioned in the mile-by-mile ride description.

Being Prepared

Mountain Biking: Colorado Springs is a *where*-to-ride book. *How* to ride is another story. However, "what to bring" lies in the gray area between the two subjects. Common sense is the rule here. Bring what makes you feel comfortable. If you need a personal mechanic to follow you, pay Bikeshop

Bob to do so. If you like riding in just shorts and a hat, well, it's your body. Here are a few ideas on tools, first-aid, clothing, altitude sickness, drinking water, and weather.

TOOLS

Tools are a touchy subject for bikers; everyone has their own opinion. When deciding how many tools to bring, I keep one question in mind. "What's the farthest I'd have to walk?" I weigh out the tools and my desire not to walk, which usually leads to the following list.

sense of humor
spare tube
patch kit
Allen wrench (pocket-knife style)
channel locks
air pump
spare cables (rear derailleur and rear brake)

If you can't replace a tube without tire levers, then bring them (learning the task will save weight and punctured tubes).

This list is too short for some and too long for others. If you get stranded remember that, with time, everywhere is within walking distance.

FIRST AID

A first-aid kit should be considered. Prevention is the first thing to put in the kit. However, if something happens, it's good to be prepared. Again, I think of one question: "How far am I from help?" Here's a partial list of things to consider.

sun screen
energy bar

butterfly-closure bandages
adhesive bandages
gauze compress pads and gauze wrap
allergy pills
emergency water purification tablets
moleskin
antiseptic swabs

The best thing to take along is usually a riding partner. Riding alone in remote areas isn't wise. If something happens, remain calm and make decisions with a clear mind. Also bear in mind the primary rule of first aid is "do no harm." This means doing only what you must to keep the injured person alive and as comfortable as possible until you can get to a doctor.

Some standard cycling apparel also makes sense from a first-aid standpoint. **Wear a helmet**. Gloves and cycling shorts are pretty much a given. Gloves will save your hands at one time or another, and cycling shorts will save your butt. Sunglasses help prevent burned-out retinas and offer some protection from dust, kamikaze insects, and rocks spun up by the knobby in front of you.

Altitude sickness shouldn't be a problem for most locals. But visitors from lower elevations may feel its effects. Headache, nausea, dizziness, and fatigue are warning signs. Also check for irregular breathing and a rapid, bounding heart rate at rest. If these symptoms don't subside, or if any one of them is severe enough to cause distress, descend to a lower elevation immediately. These relatively mild symptoms can rapidly progress to a more serious build-up of fluid in the lungs or brain, either of which can be deadly.

The best way to avoid altitude sickness is to give your body plenty of time to acclimate to higher elevations. Riders from sea level should probably take it easy the first few days in Colorado. Drink lots of water, juice, and electrolyte drinks; avoid caffeine and alcohol. A healthy diet also helps. Also remember that altitude sickness is unpredictable. It can strike anyone, even the young, healthy, and physically fit. Some people suffer mild symptoms at elevations as low as 5,000 feet. And the symptoms can strike even days after a person has apparently acclimated.

WATER

The water question is twofold: "How much do I need?" and "Where can I get more?"

The human body needs a lot of water. Experts say in summer heat a person exercising hard uses 1.5 to 2.5 gallons of water each day. That's a lot of water! And higher elevations tend to increase the need. I wear a backpack-style hydration system and keep a gallon jug in the car. I also use an electrolyte replacement drink-mix, like Gatorade.

For extremely long rides, a refill may be needed. Colorado's streams and lakes may look clear and clean, but you can't drink straight from them without treating the water first. The problem? A pesky little protozoan called Giardia lamblia. Giardia is a waterborne parasite that causes intense gastrointestinal problems. It's a bug that isn't fun to catch but is easy to avoid. *Don't drink untreated water!* Packing a purification method allows on-the-go refilling. Filters are the best way to treat backcountry water. Some cyclists like to go light and use chlorine, Halazone, or iodine tablets. These, however, are not fully reliable and may pose hazards of their own. Check with local sporting goods stores for water filters.

One other note: If creek water splashes onto a water bottle, let the bottle's water flow over the drinking spout to rinse it off before imbibing.

Weather

Mother Nature is beautiful and wonderful, but she doesn't plan weather around bike rides. Colorado's weather is notoriously unpredictable. Rain, wind, and even snow can whip up in any season. Usually this just lends a bit of adventure to the ride. But one person's adventure may be another's worst nightmare. Just remember: Panic is not a survival tool!

Thunderstorms are frequent afternoon visitors to the region. With little warning they roll in, blowing, raining, and hailing. Temperatures dip and lightning cracks. Luckily the storms pass quickly. When a storm starts forming, it's wise to turn around and head for home. If you do get caught in the open, some precautions can help keep you safe.

When you can hear thunder, you are close enough to be struck by lightning. However, you can check how close the lightning is with the old trick of counting the seconds between the flash and the thunderclap. A "five-Mississippi" count is about 1 mile. If the bolts are closer than a couple of miles, it's time to take precautions. When out in the open, ditch the bike and metal objects. Then get away. Don't be the tallest thing around and do not hide under a lone tree. The idea is to avoid being a lightning rod or hiding under one. Look for a depression or low point and crouch down. Don't lie down, and do try to avoid puddles and moving water. The water or metal objects can conduct lightning. In a forest, find shelter by moving downhill and seeking out a solid stand of smaller trees. Caves and overhangs are usually a bad idea—lightning can flash across their openings or carom inside.

The odds of getting hit by lightning are quite slim. However, they are greater than the chances of winning the Lotto. Do you play Lotto?

During a storm, temperatures usually drop dramatically. That drop paired with rain and wind means hypothermia (lowering of your core body heat) becomes a real threat. Try to keep dry and out of the wind. Exercise and an energy bar should keep you warm, but that's not a sure thing. Dress for current and predicted conditions and be ready for unexpected changes. I bring a shell to cut the wind and rain even on sunny days. Some people toss in rain pants. High-altitude rides call for cold-weather gear and possibly snow gear. Bring what makes you comfortable. Bear in mind that wet weather can make trails boggy, turning a short ride into a long (cold) one. An emergency blanket is a good idea.

Usually, the best conditions for off-road riding in the region around Colorado Springs can be found from mid-June through October. Some trails, particularly at higher elevations, have much shorter seasons, running from late July through August. (Bear in mind that hunting seasons in some areas may overlap prime pedaling times. For specific dates check with the Colorado Division of Wildlife; see Appendix B).

At any time of year, rain or snow can turn trails to purée for days afterward. Please stay off wet, muddy trails. The risk of soil damage and erosion is simply too great.

In the Colorado Springs area, North Cheyenne Canyon usually dries out early and stays ridable late into fall. Rides 1, 2, 3, 7, 8, 16, and 17 are good bets during seasonal transitions.

Woodland Park tends to get snow sooner than the Colorado Springs area. However, Mueller Park has some fabulous late fall rides. Keep an eye on the weather and check out ride 27.

Rides 35 and 36 grant Cañon City an almost year-round riding season.

The rides around San Isabel Lake usually offer great late-season action. While the area gets cold, the snow tends to hit later. Watch the weather, dress warmly, and then try rides 38, 40, 41, and 43.

The road rides in the Wet Mountain Valley are accessible year-round. The occasional blizzard will shut down the fun, but only until the plows come. See rides 44, 45, and 46.

Ridin' Right!

If every mountain biker always yielded the right-of-way, stayed on the trail, avoided wet or muddy trails, never cut switchbacks, never skidded, always rode in control, showed respect for other trail users, and carried out every last scrap of what was carried in (candy wrappers and bike-part debris included)—in short, if we all *did the right thing*—we wouldn't need a list of rules governing our behavior.

Fact is, most mountain bikers are conscientious and are trying to do the right thing. Most of us own that integrity. (No one becomes good at something as demanding and painful as grunting up sheer mountainsides by cheating.)

Most of us don't need rules.

But we do need knowledge of what exactly is the right thing to do.

Here are some guidelines—I like to think of them as reminders—reprinted by permission from the International Mountain Bicycling Association. The basic idea is to prevent or minimize damage to land, water, plants, and wildlife, and to avoid conflicts with other backcountry visitors and trail users. Ride with respect.

MULTIPLE USE TRAIL GUIDELINES
TRAIL COURTESY

YIELD TO

IMBA RULES OF THE TRAIL

Thousands of miles of dirt trails have been closed to mountain bicyclists. The irresponsible riding habits of a few riders have been a factor. Do your part to maintain trail access by observing the following rules of the trail, formulated by the International Mountain Bicycling Association (IMBA). IMBA's mission is to promote environmentally sound and socially responsible mountain biking.

1. Ride on open trails only. Respect trail and road closures (ask if not sure), avoid possible trespass on private land, obtain permits and authorization as may be required. Federal and state wilderness areas are closed to cycling. The way you ride will influence trail management decisions and policies.

2. Zero impact. Be sensitive to the dirt beneath you. Even on open (legal) trails, you should not ride under conditions where you will leave evidence of your passing, such as on certain soils after a rain. Recognize different types of soil and trail construction; practice low-impact cycling. This also means staying on existing trails and not creating any new ones. Be sure to pack out at least as much as you pack in.

3. Control your bicycle! Inattention for even a second can cause problems. Obey all bicycle speed regulations and recommendations.

4. Always yield the trail. Make known your approach well in advance. A friendly greeting (or bell) is considerate and works well; don't startle others. Show your respect when passing by, slowing to a walking pace or stopping. Anticipate other trail users at corners and blind spots.

5. Never spook animals. All animals are startled by an unannounced approach, a sudden movement, or a loud noise. This can be dangerous for you, others, and the animals. Give animals extra room and time to adjust to you. When passing horses, use special care and follow directions from the horseback riders (dismount and ask if uncertain). Running cattle and disturbing wildlife is a serious offense. Leave gates as you found them, or as marked.

6. Plan ahead. Know your equipment, your ability, and the area in which you are riding—and prepare accordingly. Be self-sufficient at all times, keep your equipment in good repair, and carry necessary supplies for changes in weather or other conditions. A well-executed trip is a satisfaction to you and not a burden or offense to others. Always wear a helmet.

Keep trails open by setting a good example of environmentally sound and socially responsible off-road cycling. Perhaps you can take it a step further and volunteer for a trail maintenance crew.

Don't let all of these precautions dampen your enthusiasm. Biking this region is great! Just pay attention to yourself, those around you, and the environment. And have fun!

Colorado Springs: High Drive Parking Lot–North Cheyenne Canyon

Many of the rides in the immediate Colorado Springs area share the High Drive parking lot as a common starting point. Some rides listed also mention parking elsewhere along the shoulder of High Drive. But this one-way road is open only in summer, so if you're riding here in spring or fall, park in the designated parking lot. All of the odometer readings for High Drive rides begin from the parking lot.

The rides are described individually, but they also work well when linked into various loops. Look at the map and refer to the mileages and difficulty ratings in each description, and then make up your own route.

ACCESS

Cheyenne Boulevard and Gold Camp Road both lead from Colorado Springs to the High Drive parking lot. From town, take Cheyenne Boulevard westbound. The street name eventually changes to Cheyenne Canyon Road. Turn right at the entrance to Seven Falls and continue up into North Cheyenne Canyon. The pavement ends at the High Drive lot. The other option from town is to head west on U.S. Highway 24 and turn left (south) onto Twenty-first Street. Then turn right onto Lower Gold Camp Road and go straight at the four-way stop. Drive past the Section 16 parking lot to an intersection with High Drive. Proceed up

Gold Camp Road, which turns to dirt and ends in the High Drive lot. Park in the shade of a tree if possible, but remember that falling sap may find its way onto your SUV's fancy paint job.

Captain Jack's

Location: North Cheyenne Canyon Park, 5 miles west of Colorado Springs.

Distance: 5.4-mile loop.

Time: 45 minutes to 1.5 hours.

Tread: 2.5 miles of singletrack and 2.9 miles of dirt road. The downhill portion of singletrack is gravelly.

Aerobic level: Moderate. Most of the climb is in the first mile.

Technical difficulty: 3, with 0.4 mile of 3+. Gravel is the main obstacle. Watch for cars in the tunnels.

Highlights: Ride this very popular singletrack in a clockwise direction! The singletrack serves up some tight turns, gravel, and vistas of the canyon and city. Watch out for motorcycles on the singletrack of this good lunch-hour choice.

Land status: North Cheyenne Canyon Park and Pike National Forest.

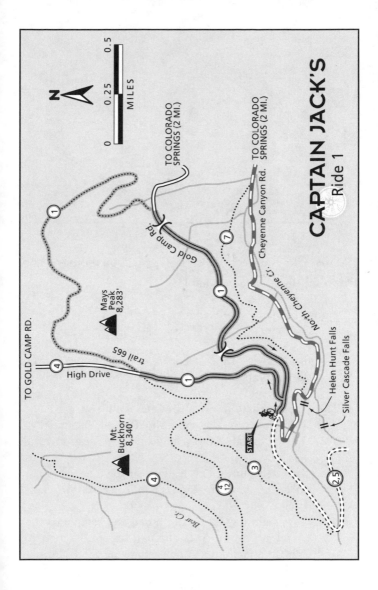

CAPTAIN JACK'S
Ride 1

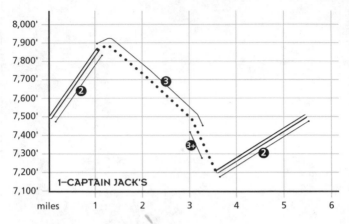

Maps: Pike National Forest; USGS Manitou Springs.

Access: High Drive parking lot.

The Ride

0.0 Leave the southeast corner of High Drive parking lot and immediately begin climbing moderately on High Drive.

1.0 Turn right onto the Penrose Multi-use Trail 665. (This junction is common to a couple of trails.)

1.2 Top of initial climb. Hang on for a long downhill run.

3.1 The trail plunges even more steeply and rates a 3+ in difficulty for the final 0.4 mile. Keep your weight back to surf the gravel.

3.5 Turn right on Gold Camp Road and begin a moderate climb to return to the parking lot. Be alert for cars in the tunnel. (This makes a good alternate trailhead.)

5.4 High Drive parking lot.

Gold Camp Road

Location: North Cheyenne Canyon Park, 5 miles west of Colorado Springs.

Distance: 29.2 miles out and back.

Time: Varies by distance. Figure about 4 hours out and back for the full distance.

Tread: 29.2 miles of dirt road in excellent shape. A short singletrack section detours around a collapsed tunnel.

Aerobic level: Easy, moderate, or strenuous. The rating of this gradual climb will depend on the distance ridden. Riding to Cripple Creek is much more strenuous than riding to the St. Mary's trailhead.

Technical difficulty: 2. Speed, gravel, and washboard-like bumps can combine to increase the rating to 3.

Highlights: A scenic and peaceful ride. Cars are forbidden on this road, creating a wide track for bikes. Views of the plains and North Cheyenne Canyon unfold beneath as the road twists into the mountains. Cars are allowed at the 8.4-mile mark (at Old Stage Road), and one day in the future cars will be granted access to all of Gold Camp Road as they had in the past. Gold Camp Road links with Jones's Downhill (ride 12), Mount Baldy (ride 11), and St. Mary's Falls (ride 5).

Land status: Pike National Forest.

Maps: Pike National Forest; USGS Manitou Springs and Mount Big Chief.

Access: High Drive parking lot.

The Ride

0.0 Leave the High Drive parking lot via the closed portion of Gold Camp Road marked by a large green gate

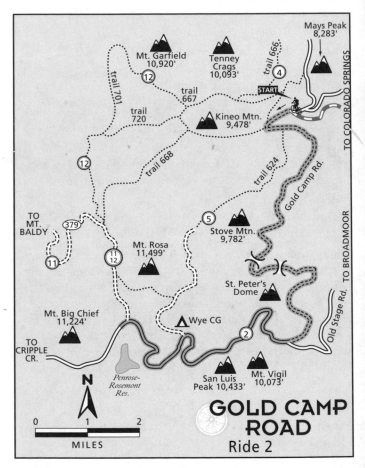

on the northwest corner of the lot. The road climbs steadily at a moderate clip of about 180 feet per mile.

1.1 Turn left onto the St. Mary's Trail. This is a detour for the collapsed tunnel.

1.2 Take the left fork and return to the road. The St. Mary's Trail continues to the right (see ride 5).

4.8 The first of two tunnels. Bring a light if you have issues with the dark.

8.4 Turn right as Old Stage Road merges with Gold Camp Road. Cars are allowed from this point onward. Left returns to Colorado Springs near the Cheyenne Mountain Zoo.

8.8 Keep right on Gold Camp Road.

9.3 Stay left on Gold Camp Road.

12.4 Pass Wye Campground off to the right. The grade eases.

14.6 Junction with Mount Baldy Road (Forest Road 379) on right. Decision time! Turn around for a great downhill run back to the High Drive parking lot; or turn right onto FR 379 for Jones's Downhill (see ride 12) and the area's best singletrack downhill.

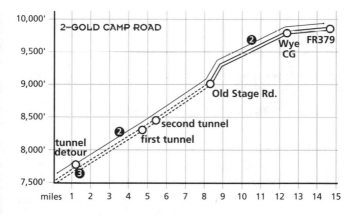

Either way returns to the High Drive parking lot. True mileage junkies can stay left on Gold Camp Road and pedal another 20 miles to Colorado Highway 67 and the town of Cripple Creek (arrange a vehicle shuttle beforehand—you may be able to convince a casino shuttle to get you home).

Buckhorn Loop
(Captain Jack's Frontside)

Location: North Cheyenne Canyon Park, 5 miles west of Colorado Springs.

Distance: 3.9-mile loop.

Time: 30 to 45 minutes.

Tread: 2.2 miles of singletrack and 1.7 miles of dirt road. The hard-packed, dirt singletrack is in good shape, but the last 0.5 mile on trail 667 has loose gravel.

Aerobic level: Moderate. The singletrack is a fairly constant climb.

Technical difficulty: 3. Surf is in the form of roots, rocks, and gravel.

Highlights: Buckhorn is a great "quick fix" that lunch-hour commandos will want on their menus. Just enough uphill to pump the legs, plenty of downhill, and some

24

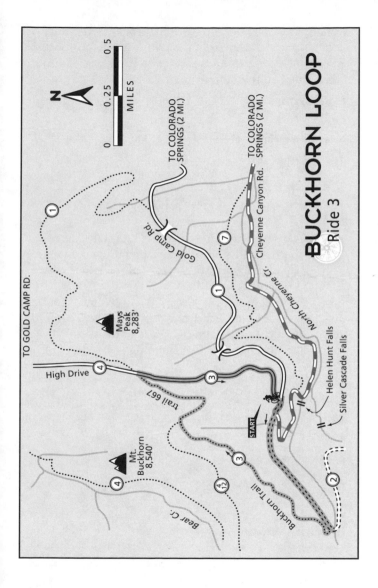

BUCKHORN LOOP
Ride 3

N

0   0.25   0.5

MILES

TO GOLD CAMP RD.

Mays Peak
8,283'

High Drive

trail 667

Mt. Buckhorn
8,540'

Bear C.

Buckhorn Trail

START

Helen Hunt Falls

Silver Cascade Falls

Cheyenne Canyon Rd.

North Cheyenne C.

Gold Camp Rd.

TO COLORADO
SPRINGS (2 MI.)

TO COLORADO
SPRINGS (2 MI.)

technical sections to keep the brain awake. Ride clockwise or be prepared to leap from the trail to avoid other cyclists. You'll get nasty looks and load up on bad karma if you run other riders off their climb.

Land status: Pike National Forest and North Cheyenne Canyon Park.

Maps: Pike National Forest; USGS Manitou Springs.

Access: High Drive parking lot.

The Ride

- **0.0** Leave the High Drive parking lot via the closed portion of Gold Camp Road marked by a large green gate on the northwest corner of the lot. The road is closed to cars, not bikes.
- **0.6** Turn right on Buckhorn Trail directly before the sweeping, left-hand hairpin turn. (Watch for this discreet trail on the right side of the road, 30 yards after a small metal sign stating NO VEHICLE USE OFF

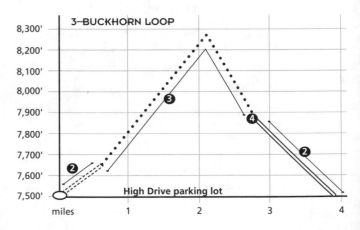

THIS ROAD, and about the same distance before the sign for North Cheyenne Creek.)

0.7 After this first pitch there is a switchback and a trail to the left. Keep right and follow the switchback. The left trail is the Seven Bridges trail (see ride 6).

2.0 Turn right at the T junction onto the Jones Park Multi-use Trail 667. Left leads down to the Bear Creek Trail (see ride 4) or up to Jones Park (see ride 12).

2.8 Turn right on High Drive and descend to the parking lot. This junction also connects to three other rides: Either cross the road to Trail 665 (see ride 1), or turn left and descend to the Palmer Trail (see ride 9) or the Intemann Trail (see ride 10).

3.9 High Drive parking lot.

Bear Creek Loop

Location: 3 miles west of Colorado Springs and 2 miles south of Manitou Springs.

Distance: 8.3 miles

Time: 1.5 hours.

Tread: 3.5 miles of singletrack, 4.2 miles of dirt road, and 0.6 mile of paved road. Loose gravel is prevalent in Bear Canyon.

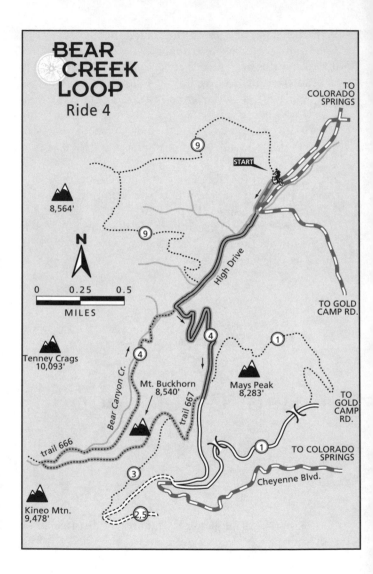

BEAR CREEK LOOP
Ride 4

TO COLORADO SPRINGS

⑨

START

8,564'

N

⑨

0   0.25   0.5
MILES

High Drive

TO GOLD CAMP RD.

Tenney Crags
10,093'

④

①

Bear Canyon Cr.

Mt. Buckhorn
8,540'

trail 667

Mays Peak
8,283'

④

TO GOLD CAMP RD.

trail 666

①

TO COLORADO SPRINGS

Kineo Mtn.
9,478'

③

2.5

Cheyenne Blvd.

Aerobic level: Moderate. The ride starts with an 1,800-foot climb in under 4 miles. Starting at the High Drive parking lot avoids the initial climb but leaves a steep climb at the end of the ride.

Technical difficulty: 3+. The surf gets a bit rough in Bear Canyon in the form of loose gravel.

Highlights: The downhill section is scenic and exhilarating. In Bear Canyon loose gravel and occasional rocks paired with distracting views can endo the best riders. Stop as needed to admire the view and then hang on to enjoy the thrill ride down. Watch for car traffic on High Drive. You can link this ride to the Intemann Trail (ride 10) or the Pikes Peak Greenway (ride 24).

Land status: Bear Creek Canyon Park and Pike National Forest.

Maps: Pike National Forest; USGS Manitou Springs.

Access: Park in the Section 16 lot. From Colorado Springs, drive west on U.S. Highway 24 and turn left onto Twenty-first Street. Then turn right onto Lower Gold Camp Road. Continue straight at the four-way stop. The Section 16

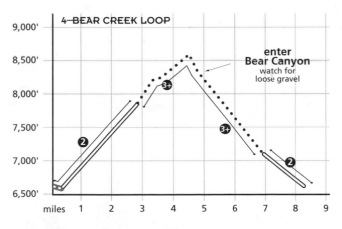

parking lot is on the right with additional parking just
down the road. In summer, parking is allowed on High Drive.

The Ride

0.0 From the Section 16 parking lot head west up Gold
Camp Road.

0.3 Turn right at the all-way stop sign and cross the gate
for High Drive. If it's closed for the season, use the
small step on the side. Continue the moderate climb
up High Drive.

1.0 The Palmer Trail (see ride 9) leaves on the right;
stay on the road.

1.4 The Lower Bear Creek Trail meets the road here on
the right; stay on the road as it bends left.

2.8 Turn right at the top of High Drive onto the Jones
Park Trail 667. This is a busy section of trail with
two-way traffic, including riders on Captain Jack's
(see ride 1). Another option is to roll down to the
High Drive parking lot, follow ride 3 to its 2.0 mile
mark, and turn left (see ride 3).

3.6 The trail forks; keep right on the Jones Park Trail.
The Buckhorn Trail (see ride 3) descends on the
left.

4.8 Turn right onto the appropriately numbered Trail
666 and hold on for the wild ride down Bear
Canyon. Watch for loose gravel.

6.9 Retrace the route to the parking lot by turning left
on High Drive.

8.3 Section 16 parking lot.

5

St. Mary's Falls

Location: North Cheyenne Canyon, 5 miles west of Colorado Springs.

Distance: 7.3 miles one-way to Mount Baldy Road; or do a 16.8-mile loop by taking Jones's Downhill (see ride 12).

Time: 3 hours out and back. The loop takes 4 hours.

Tread: 4.9 miles of singletrack and 2.4 miles of dirt road. Erosion has rutted the beginning of the dirt road and a downed tree crosses the upper singletrack.

Aerobic level: Strenuous. This ride in its entirety is not for the timid. Its rating stems more from the length of the entire ascent rather than steepness. But it is very steep by the falls.

Technical difficulty: 3+. Tight switchbacks and eroding steeps create some sections of class 4 riding, which often turns into a "hike-a-bike" experience.

Highlights: This ride starts with a mild ascent through pine, spruce, and aspen with Buffalo Creek in sight. In fact, many people ride just this stretch and return. Grunt out the steeps by St. Mary's Falls to ride through the tailings of an old mine. From here the ride is moderate. The trail to Mount Baldy Road offers narrow singletrack and more glimpses of Colorado's mining past. St. Mary's does have a lot of unmarked side trails, making route finding difficult. No worries if a turn is missed, though, just more work. This is a fun out-and-back or a loop with Gold Camp Road (see ride 2), or Jones's Downhill (see ride 12).

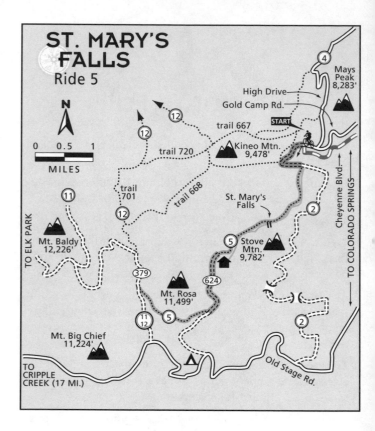

Land status: Pike National Forest. A short section near Mount Baldy Road skirts private land.

Maps: Pike National Forest; USGS Manitou Springs, Big Chief.

Access: High Drive parking lot.

The Ride

0.0 Leave the High Drive parking lot via the closed portion of Gold Camp Road marked by a large green gate on the northwest corner of the lot. The road is closed to cars but not bikes.

0.6 Pass by the Buckhorn Loop and Seven Bridges Trail. Stay on the main road.

1.1 The tunnel here has collapsed. The main route now detours onto the St. Mary's Trail. Leave the road on the left and climb above the tunnel.

1.2 At the fork, turn right. A sign for the falls (1.75 miles ahead) marks the way.

2.4 Junction; keep right. A metal sign gives the distance to the falls as 0.2 mile.

2.6 Again, keep right at the sign. Left goes to the falls.

3.2 Keep right. Left heads to the creek.

3.5 Keep right as the trail becomes an old doubletrack.

3.9 Right at the fork to a steep, rocky incline.

4.0 Keep left as a road joins from the right.

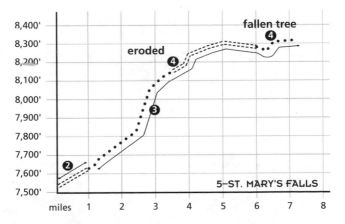

4.6 An old mine lies on this eroded hill with lots of intersecting roads. The proper road is labeled 624. Keep on this main road and enjoy some downhill.

6.2 Go straight across the intersection marked on the left with a small cement structure. In about 10 meters leave Road 624 for the trail on the right. A marker for Road 624 stands beside the trail but points to the road.

6.4 Turn right after a short, steep downhill where a singletrack leaves the road. The area is recognizable by three dead stumps. Take the singletrack and immediately cross a trickling stream.

6.6 A fallen tree impedes the way. Heavy surf, dude!

7.3 Junction with Mount Baldy Road (FR 379). To create a loop, turn right onto Mount Baldy Road and pedal 1 mile onto Jones's Downhill (see ride 12). Left continues on to Gold Camp Road (see ride 2).

6

Seven Bridges Trail

Location: North Cheyenne Canyon Park

Distance: 3.9 miles one way.

Time: 1.5 hours.

Tread: 3.9 miles of singletrack that ranges from packed dirt to loose gravel. If you get off the main route at mile 1.7 you'll experience loose gravel like you've never experienced

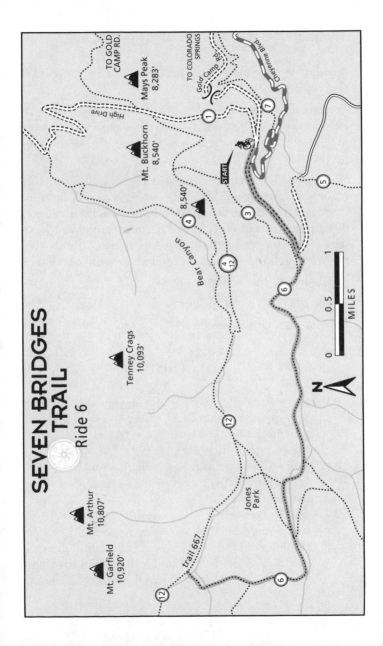

SEVEN BRIDGES TRAIL
Ride 6

Mt. Garfield 10,920'

Mt. Arthur 10,807'

Tenney Crags 10,093'

trail 667

Jones Park

Mays Peak 8,283'

TO GOLD CAMP RD.

TO COLORADO SPRINGS

Gold Camp Rd.

Cheyenne Blvd.

High Drive

Mt. Buckhorn 8,540'

8,540'

Bear Canyon

START

N

MILES
0   0.5   1

before! It's not a good thing. Pay attention and stay on route.

Aerobic level: Strenuous. The climb is constant—make that relentless.

Technical difficulty: 4+. Actually, much of the trail is 3+. However, the bridges are class 5 trials moves. The loose gravel on steep sections also is a technically challenging proposition.

Highlights: The technical difficulty of this trail is the main highlight. After the bridges, the route heads away from the creek and into a peaceful forest setting. Actually, the setting doesn't change. But you can pay attention to the surroundings more after you pass the bridges. This is the shortest route to reach the upper end of Jones's Downhill (ride 12).

Land status: Pike National Forest

Maps: USGS Manitou Springs.

Access: High Drive parking lot.

The Ride

0.0 Leave the High Drive parking lot via the closed portion of Gold Camp Road marked by a large green gate on the northwest corner of the lot. The road is closed to cars, not bikes.

0.6 Stay on the road as it passes by the Buckhorn Trail. (Buckhorn is directly before the sweeping, left-hand hairpin turn.)

0.7 The Seven Bridges Trail leaves the road to the right in the middle of the sweeping turn. You'll have to climb up over some roots on a short ramp up to the trail then cross the first bridge. If this doesn't ring a bell then you may have exited the road on the Buck-

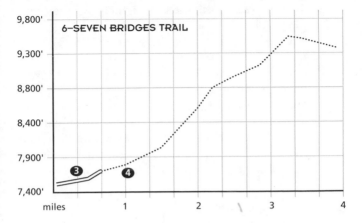

6–SEVEN BRIDGES TRAIL

horn Trail. If you did, take the first left at the switchback and you'll be delivered to the Seven Bridges Trail past bridge one.

1.0 Keep crossing bridges.

1.7 The route starts to bear ever-so-slightly right up the canyon's righthand slope. As the trail exits the trees into a long, granite, scree slide, be sure to keep as far right as possible. A false trail runs nearer the water and is a hike-a-bike nightmare. The tread on the correct trail is gravel and pretty loose, but not nearly as loose as if you stayed down near the creek. If it gets downright cussingly loose then you're probably off the route. Either slug ahead or backtrack. If you slug ahead, you'll have to carry your bike and scramble a bit, but eventually you'll find a trail to rejoin the route after it re-enters the trees.

2.3 Y intersection. Stay right. Left heads 2.6 miles up Trail 668 to Frosty Park and the Jones's Downhill and Mount Baldy rides (rides 11 and 12).

2.5 Keep left as a trail leaves up to the right.

2.8 T intersection. Keep left. A right turn heads into Jones Park.

2.85 Keep right as a trail enters from the left. The left trail joins the route that separated from this description at mile 2.3. This route will climb a bit more before bending to the north.

3.4 Stay right as Trail 720 enters on the left.

3.9 T intersection with Trail 667. A right turn will get you back to your car via Jones's Downhill (ride 12). Just be sure and turn on Trail 667 when it climbs away from Trail 666 to join the Buckhorn Trail.

Columbine

Location: North Cheyenne Canyon, 3 miles west of Colorado Springs.

Distance: 3.8 miles one way.

Time: 1 hour.

Tread: Wide singletrack the whole way. Surf is up with sections of loose gravel.

Aerobic level: Strenuous due to loose gravel climbs.

Technical difficulty: 3. The switchbacks paired with loose gravel are tricky.

Highlights: The Columbine trail offers spectacular vistas of the canyon and the Broadmoor below. The rock walls and

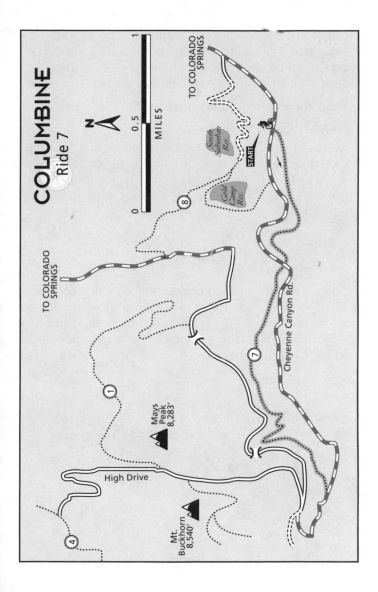

ledges are divine during wildflower season. Look for columbine, Colorado's state flower. There was talk of closing this crowded trail to bikes but at press time it was still open. Columbine loops well with The Chutes (see ride 8).

Land status: North Cheyenne Canyon Park.

Maps: USGS Manitou Springs.

Access: Take Cheyenne Boulevard westbound to North Cheyenne Park. Keep right on Cheyenne at the entrance to Seven Falls. Park at the trailhead, less than 0.1 mile up the road on the left. There is also a parking lot at the Discovery Center.

The Ride

0.0 The singletrack, marked with a small sign, leaves from the left side of the small parking area. Immediately cross the creek and climb a short hill to a picnic area. The singletrack here is 5 feet wide, hard packed, and level.

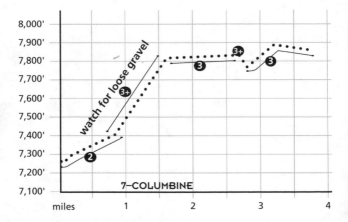

0.25 Continue straight through two more picnic areas. The old stonework in the stream is a gaging station.

0.5 Turn left at the trail marker as you leave this last picnic area. The trail has a switchback and becomes level, skirting a narrow ledge and rock wall.

0.8 Cross a wide bridge and STOP before crossing Cheyenne Canyon Road, which is a busy road. The trail is easily picked up on the other side.

1.0 The middle trailhead.

1.1 Loose gravel marks the start of some 3+ switchbacks that quickly gain elevation.

1.4 An old trail leading away to the left is closed; bear right. The gradient eases.

2.8 Keep right after going down some tight switchbacks and through some large rocks. The small trail on the left is closed. The main trail then climbs again.

3.8 Upper trailhead. To connect to other trails turn right and climb 0.5 mile. Grab a look at the map and pick a trail. A good loop back to the car is The Chutes (ride 8).

The Chutes

Location: 2 miles west of Colorado Springs.

Distance: 2.1 miles one way.

Time: 45 minutes up; 15 minutes down.

Tread: 1.1 miles of hard-packed singletrack, 1.1 miles of dirt road, and 0.9 mile of paved road.

Aerobic level: Moderate. This ride is short but fairly steep.

Technical difficulty: 3. The bermed corners on the way down add a bit to the difficulty and the fun.

Highlights: This ride's bermed turns give the downhill a bobsled feel. Too bad it's so short. Watch for people making the climb while going downhill! Combine this with the Columbine Trail (see ride 7) for a great loop. The Stratton Open Space has developed new trails in recent years. Weave among the pines and gamble oak before heading up the Chutes to add distance and nature to your ride.

Land status: North Cheyenne Mountain Park and private holdings.

Maps: USGS Colorado Springs. The junction of The Chutes and Gold Camp Road is on the Manitou Springs quad.

Access: Take Cheyenne Boulevard westbound to Ridgeway Road and turn right. This road leads to a developed trailhead on the left. Another trailhead lies farther down Cheyenne Boulevard just past the entrance to Seven Falls.

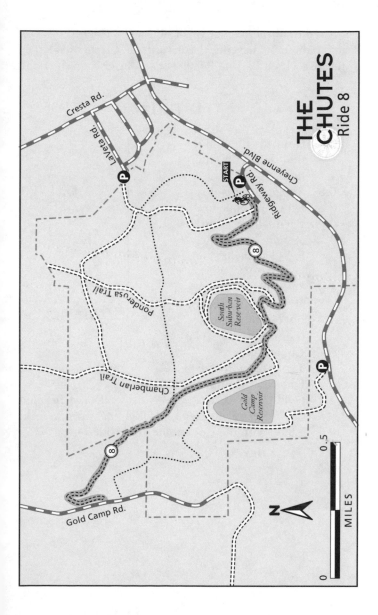

THE
CHUTES Ride 8

Cresta Rd.

Laveta Rd.

Cheyenne Blvd.

Ridgeway Rd.

START

Ponderosa Trail

Chamberlan Trail

South
Suburban
Reservoir

Gold Camp
Reservoir

Gold Camp Rd.

8

8

N

MILES

0   0.5

A third trailhead, the La Veta trailhead, is reached by turning right off Cheyenne Boulevard on Cresta Road then turning left on La Veta Road. The trailhead is on the right.

The Ride

0.0 Head up the Chutes trail from the trailhead.

0.8 The road forks. Keep left at this junction.

0.9 Keep left as the trail around South Suburban Reservoir joins on the right.

1.0 Take the middle fork at this three-way intersection (follow the sign for The Chutes).

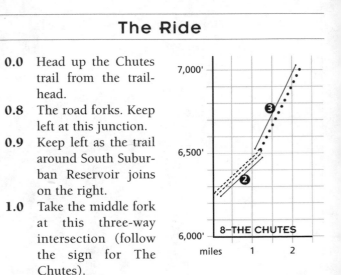

1.9 The trail switchbacks left. Stay on the main track, ignoring the minor trail to the right.

2.1 Gold Camp Road. Retrace your tracks to Cheyenne Boulevard, or turn left on Gold Camp Road to make a loop with the Columbine Trail (ride 7).

Palmer Trail– Section 16 Loop

Location: 3 miles west of Colorado Springs and 2 miles south of Manitou Springs.

Distance: 5.8-mile loop.

Time: 1.5 hours.

Tread: 4.8 miles of singletrack, 0.8 mile of dirt road, and 0.2 mile of paved road. Expect good conditions with the exception of Section 16, which resembles a steep, empty streambed.

Aerobic level: Moderate.

Technical difficulty: 3, but the upper portion of the Section 16 downhill rates a 5+.

Highlights: Old pine forests, tumbling streams, and ruins keep the mind off the gradual climb. The view from the top of the Crystal Park spur is spectacular, but stop before the Crystal Park subdivision. Many riders stick to the Palmer Trail for an out-and-back ride because erosion has made the Section 16 descent treacherous. It's basically a steep wash that challenges even the best riders.

Land status: Bear Creek Canyon Park and Pike National Forest.

Maps: Pike National Forest; USGS Manitou Springs.

Access: From Colorado Springs drive west on U.S. Highway 24 and turn left onto Twenty-first Street. Then turn

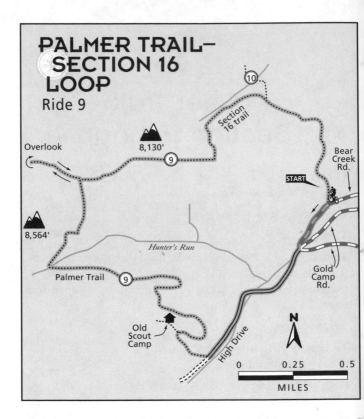

PALMER TRAIL–SECTION 16 LOOP
Ride 9

Overlook

8,130'

Section 16 trail

10

9

Bear Creek Rd.

START

8,564'

Hunter's Run

Palmer Trail 9

Gold Camp Rd.

Old Scout Camp

High Drive

N

0   0.25   0.5
MILES

right onto Lower Gold Camp Road. Continue straight at the four-way stop. The Section 16 parking lot is on the right with additional parking just down the road. In summer parking is allowed on High Drive, which leaves an uphill finish.

The Ride

0.0 From the Section 16 trailhead parking lot, head west on Gold Camp Road.

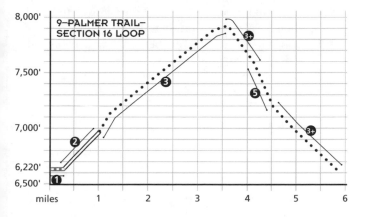

9–PALMER TRAIL–
SECTION 16 LOOP

0.3 Turn right at the all-way stop sign and cross the gate for High Drive. If it's closed for the season, use the steps on the side.

0.9 A trail comes off the road at a 30-degree angle. This is an alternate trailhead. The official one is just ahead.

1.0 Turn right at the small, rusty metal gate marking the trailhead proper. The alternate trail joins in 0.1 mile ahead.

1.2 Turn right, doubling back on a switchback. Another trail continues ahead to an old scout camp. All that remains is a chimney and the foundation to the wash house.

3.3 Decision time. The loop—and this description—turns right to Section 16. It gets very technical. The left fork ascends toward Crystal Park and a wonderful view of the Garden of the Gods. Going left, it's 0.3 mile to the overlook and the end of the trail at a private property line. Any farther is trespassing.

4.0 Turn left at this small fork and head down. The right simply peters out at a small overlook.

4.1 The trail descends a wash. Loose gravel and rocks abound. A technical rating of 5+!

4.5 This small clearing can be confusing. Follow the trail to the right and down.

4.9 Pass by the Paul Intemann Memorial Trail (see ride 10). The tread gets easier from here. But keep awake for rock drop-offs and people.

5.8 Back at the parking lot.

Paul Intemann Memorial Trail–Southern Segment

Location: 3 miles west of Colorado Springs and 2 miles south of Manitou Springs.

Distance: 5 miles out and back.

Time: 1 hour.

Tread: 5 miles of singletrack.

Aerobic level: Mostly easy. Only a few brief climbs.

Technical difficulty: 4. Tight, rocky switchbacks on this one!

Highlights: An excellent technical test! Many different obstacles make a clean ride tough. Unfortunately the trail isn't complete. It's scheduled to connect to Manitou

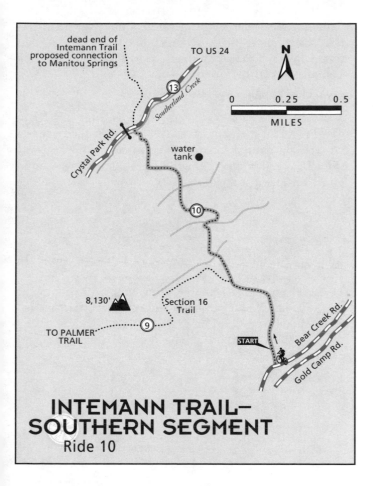

dead end of
Intemann Trail
proposed connection
to Manitou Springs

TO US 24

N

Southerland Creek

13

0   0.25   0.5
MILES

Crystal Park Rd.

water
tank

10

8,130'

Section 16
Trail

9

TO PALMER
TRAIL

START

Bear Creek Rd.

Gold Camp Rd.

INTEMANN TRAIL–
SOUTHERN SEGMENT
Ride 10

Springs. For now, it ends shortly after crossing Crystal Park
Road. A detour (see ride 13) connects to the hilly Manitou
Springs portion of the trail to ultimately deposit riders at
Iron Springs. There are some log steps along the route that
force many riders to dismount. Watch for sharp rocks and
cactus.

Land status: A variety of private holdings surround this ride. A sign marks the gap in the trail. Do not trespass past this point. For more information on the Intemann Trail Committee, check www. intemann-trail.com.

Maps: USGS Manitou Springs.

Access: From Colorado Springs drive west on U.S. Highway 24 and turn left onto Twenty-first Street. Turn right on Lower Gold Camp Road. Continue straight at the four-way stop. The Section 16 parking lot is on the right with additional parking just down the road.

The Ride

- **0.0** Begin climbing on the Section 16 trail from the parking lot.
- **0.7** The well-marked Intemann Trail leads off to the right, climbing for another 0.2 mile and then twisting downhill for more than a mile.
- **2.2** Crystal Park Road. The trail picks up again just

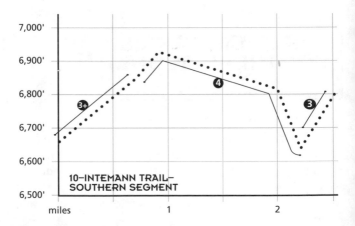

down the road to the right. However, it only goes another 0.3 mile before dead-ending. To add to the trouble, the trail at this point has a long series of stairs and tight switchbacks. You could skip this last segment and use Crystal Road as the turnaround point. Or you could ride the Manitou Springs portion of the Intemann Trail. To do so, turn right onto Crystal Park Road (see ride 13).

2.5 One last sign marks the end of the trail.

Mount Baldy

Location: 15 miles west of Colorado Springs.

Distance: 12.2 miles out and back.

Time: 2.5 hours.

Tread: 12.2 miles of four-wheel-drive road with patches of sand and loose gravel.

Aerobic level: Strenuous. The trail climbs constantly from its beginning elevation of 9,800 feet to its end at 11,840 feet. The return descent has a tendency to leave arms and legs aching for home.

Technical difficulty: 2+. This is a pretty straightforward trail. Its main difficulties come from the sandy patches. Momentum and weight distribution are the key. High downhill speed warrants a 3 rating for the return segment.

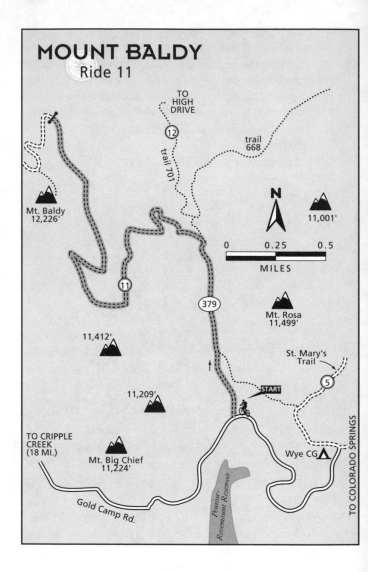

MOUNT BALDY
Ride 11

TO HIGH DRIVE

12

trail 701

trail 668

Mt. Baldy
12,226'

11,001'

N

0   0.25   0.5

MILES

11

379

Mt. Rosa
11,499'

11,412'

St. Mary's Trail

11,209'

5

START

TO CRIPPLE CREEK
(18 MI.)

Mt. Big Chief
11,224'

Wye CG

TO COLORADO SPRINGS

Gold Camp Rd.

Primrose Rosemount Reservoir

Highlights: The view from the top is one of the best in the neighborhood. Kansas is visible to the east, Pikes Peak looms in the north, and the short alpine wildflower season delivers a rare treat in early summer. The downhill is fun, but soft spots and a few water bars can make things a bit hairy. A gate at the top of the ride marks land managed by the Colorado Springs Water Department.

Land status: Pike National Forest and Colorado Springs Water Department. Bikers must stop at the gate short of the summit. In the future, the city water department may allow bikers.

Maps: Pike National Forest; USGS Manitou Springs.

Access: This ride is accessed off the Old Stage Road out of the Broadmoor. From Colorado Springs drive south on Colorado Highway 115 to CO 122 and turn right. This road becomes Lake Avenue. Keep right on Lake Avenue and circumnavigate the Broadmoor. Turn left on El Pomar Park Road and follow the signs toward the zoo. This road changes names a couple of times but is easily followed. Look for Old Stage Road to fork away to the right as the left

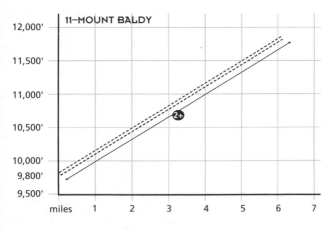

fork goes to the zoo. This junction is at Cheyenne Mountain and Penrose Boulevards. The road winds and turns to dirt in about 1 mile. Stay right at the first fork (2.5 miles from pavement's end). Again, keep right where the road to Emerald Ranch enters in (4 miles from the end of pavement). Stay on the main road, pass the Wye Campground, and park at Mount Baldy Road (Forest Road 379) in the Penrose-Rosemount Reservoir parking area on the left (12.2 miles from pavement's end).

The Ride

0.0 Start up FR 379 and immediately begin to climb to the north. The climb is consistent and the surface good. A few roads and trails join the main road. Stay on the main road.

1.7 Stay on the main road. The trail on the right is Jones's Downhill (see ride 12).

4.3 Take the right fork. The left fork heads over to Elk Park.

6.1 End of the line. The road continues ahead, but for now it's closed to bikes. Check with the Colorado Springs Water Department (719–636–5616) for current status.

12

Jones's Downhill

Location: 15 miles southwest of the Broadmoor.

Distance: 10.2 miles one way. This ride, as described, involves shuttling vehicles.

Time: 2 hours plus sightseeing time.

Tread: 8.5 miles of singletrack and 1.7 miles of four-wheel-drive road. New construction in the Jones Park region has softened the tread.

Aerobic level: Moderate. Yup, it's nearly all downhill and still ranks as moderate.

Technical difficulty: 3+. Water bars, rocky patches, and new construction all combine with speed for this rating.

Highlights: Downhill, downhill, and more downhill! Whoop-te-doos in the middle of aspen groves and Jones Park make for the ultimate downhill run in the area. Simply point the tires down the fall line. All the side trails funnel back to Trail 667 or 668. As described here, this ride ends at the High Drive parking lot. But many other options exist. Bring the maps and invent a new combination. This trail makes an excellent downhill leg for Gold Camp Road or St. Mary's Trail (see rides 2 and 5). Note: The Forest Service has found areas along this route that have been altered by bikers to "enhance" their riding experience. If you are caught doing this, you will face fines and imprisonment. A better idea is to join a trail building organization and get your ideas heard. Stay on the trail so we can keep it open to bikes.

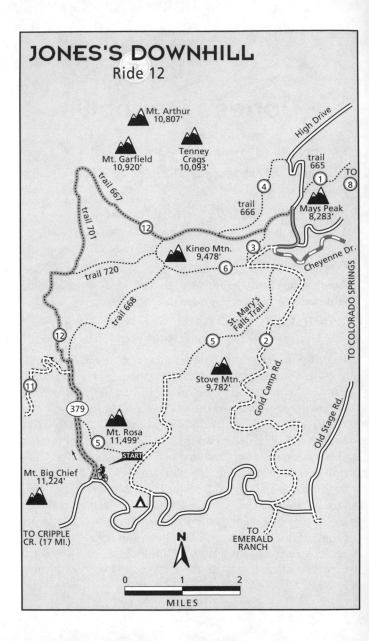

JONES'S DOWNHILL
Ride 12

Mt. Arthur
10,807'

Mt. Garfield
10,920'

Tenney
Crags
10,093'

High Drive

trail
665

trail 667

trail
666

Mays Peak
8,283'

TO
8

trail 701

12

Kineo Mtn.
9,478'

3

Cheyenne Dr.

4

1

6

trail 720

TO COLORADO SPRINGS

trail 668

St. Mary's
Falls Trail

12

5

2

Gold Camp Rd.

11

Stove Mtn.
9,782'

379

Mt. Rosa
11,499'

5

Old Stage Rd.

START

Mt. Big Chief
11,224'

TO CRIPPLE
CR. (17 MI.)

TO
EMERALD
RANCH

N

0   1   2

MILES

Land status: Pike National Forest.

Maps: Pike National Forest; USGS Manitou Springs.

Access: This ride is accessed off of the Old Stage Road out of the Broadmoor. From Colorado Springs drive south on Colorado 115 and turn right onto CO 122. This road becomes Lake Avenue. Keep right on Lake Avenue and circumnavigate the Broadmoor. Turn left on El Pomar Park Road and follow the signs toward the zoo. This road changes names a couple of times but is easily followed. Look for Old Stage Road to fork to the right as the left fork goes to the zoo. This junction is at Cheyenne Mountain and Penrose Boulevards. The road winds and turns to dirt in about 1 mile. Stay right at the first fork (2.5 miles from pavement's end). Again, keep right where the road to Emerald Ranch enters (4 miles from the end of the pavement). Stay on the main road, pass the Wye Campground, and park at Mount Baldy Road (Forest Road 379) in the Penrose-Rosemount Reservoir parking area on the left (12.2 miles from pavement's end). If the shuttle vehicle has four-wheel drive, continue up FR 379 to Trail 701.

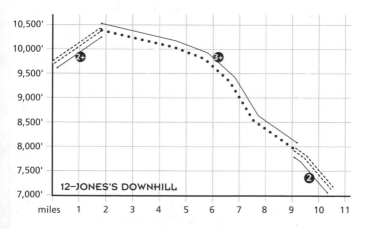

57

The Ride

0.0   Head up FR 379 and stay on it. St. Mary's Trail (ride 5) joins in from across the creek at 0.7 mile.

1.7   Turn right onto Trail 701 and begin the roller coaster downhill. (FR 379 continues to the top of Mount Baldy; see ride 11.)

1.8   Trail 668 is on the right; stay straight on Trail 701.

4.4   Continue straight ahead. The Forester Cutoff, Trail 720, heads away to the right.

5.5   Turn right onto Trail 667 (the Jones Park Trail). A left turn here leads up to Lake Moraine.

6.4   Keep left on Trail 667 and enter Jones Park. Watch for an old mine about 0.4 mile ahead. Ride 6 joins the route.

7.3   Trail 666, Beaver Creek (ride 4), continues its descent. This ride turns right and climbs briefly, continuing on Trail 667.

9.2   Turn right on High Drive. Ride 1 goes straight ahead and ride 9 is to the left.

10.2   High Drive parking lot. Continue east on Gold Camp Road to reach ride 8, The Chutes, for a route into Colorado Springs.

Paul Intemann
Memorial Trail–Manitou
Springs Segment

Location: Manitou Springs, west of Colorado Springs.

Distance: 5.1 miles (including detour) one way to the southern segment of the Intemann Trail.

Time: 1 hour.

Tread: The easternmost portion is a wide gravel trail. Through Manitou Springs the route alternates between rural roads and wide singletrack. The "Steve Beisel Detour" connects to ride 10 in this book via paved roads.

Aerobic level: Strenuous. The hills here are steep. However, most are on good surfaces, with the exception of the grind out of Iron Springs.

Technical difficulty: 3. The main hazard is loose gravel.

Highlights: This is the eastern portion of what could be an awesome trail from Gold Camp Road to the Barr Trail (ride 14). Unfortunately, when Steve Beisel bought a chunk of land south of the cemetery in Manitou Springs, negotiations took an endo. The two existing sections of the Intemann Trail can be connected via the detour described below, which adds a lot of climbing. From Iron Springs, the trail climbs the side of Red Mountain, giving views of Manitou Springs before descending to dodge through the

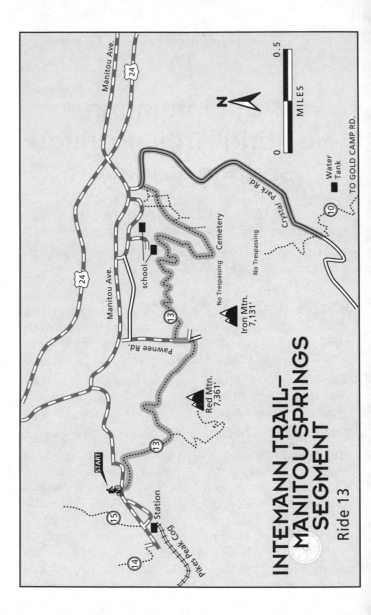

INTEMANN TRAIL—
MANITOU SPRINGS
SEGMENT
Ride 13

Manitou Ave.

24

Manitou Ave.

24

Pawnee Rd.

13

13

school

Cemetery

Crystal Park Rd.

No Trespassing

No Trespassing

Iron Mtn.
7,131'

Red Mtn.
7,361'

START

15

14

Station

Pikes Peak Cog

Water Tank

10

TO GOLD CAMP RD.

N

MILES

0   0.5

community's homes that cling to the steep hillside. The last bit runs along the hill behind the middle and high schools to end at the cemetery.

Land status: Intemann Trail Committee, www.intemann-trail.com. The open portions are owned by El Paso County and private land owners. The area you can't cross is owned by Steve Beisel, who has contacted many organizations to make sure the word gets out that you can't cross his land.

Maps: USGS Manitou Springs.

Access: From Colorado Springs take U.S. Highway 24 to Manitou Springs. Exit on the U.S. 24 business loop (Monument Avenue), turn right, and follow the signs to the Pikes Peak Cog Railway. Turn left on Ruxton Avenue to travel south from downtown and follow it past the railway depot. You will have passed by the Iron Springs trailhead. However, it is on the other side (left side) of this narrow road. Keep right as the road splits into two one-ways, then turn left where the one-ways re-join. In effect you've made a big U-turn. Now look for the trailhead on the right.

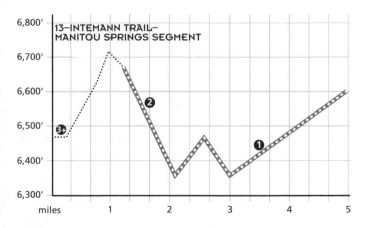

The Ride

0.0   The trail crosses the creek and follows it downstream to a bridge that requires Hans Rey skills or a dismount.

0.2   After the bridge, turn right on the road.

0.3   A sign marks the next right, which leads up to a small gravel parking area. Now comes the grinding climb up loose gravel.

0.6   Jim Gilliam bench. Ahead is a brief downhill then up to the Red Mountain Trail junction.

0.9   Keep left along the cliffside avoiding the road down to the right. The route now winds around the hill and descends to Pawnee Avenue.

1.3   Head down Pawnee Avenue to Southside Road (second right) and turn right. The road ends in a trail marked with an Intemann Trail sign, which explains the route through the neighborhood. The route rejoins the trail proper south of the middle school and works its way back to the cemetary.

2.6   Enter the cemetary and exit out the main gate. Follow Plainview Place down Poplar Place to Crystal Park Road just before it rejoins Monument Avenue. Turn right. This is the "Steve Beisel Detour," which follows Crystal Park Road uphill.

5.1   The Crystal Park trailhead (not much of a trailhead). The trail crosses the road, and there's a wide area to park in. You can turn right to overlook the area beyond which is off-limits to bikes or turn left and ride along the other half of the Paul Intemann Memorial Trail (ride 10).

Barr Trail

Location: Manitou Springs.

Distance: 11.7 miles one way.

Time: Plan at least 2 hours to reach Barr Camp. The downhill takes about 1 hour, depending on traffic.

Tread: 11.7 miles of singletrack.

Aerobic level: Strenuous. Strenuous is an understatement if ridden from the bottom. Riding down is aerobically easy.

Technical difficulty: 4-. The main obstacle is the climb. However, those who brave the upper 5 miles will find obstacles, tight switchbacks, and portages.

Highlights: While most folks will want to turn around at Barr Camp, it's theoretically possible to ride to the summit. The toll road (not open to bikes) goes to the summit for those who find a willing friend to drive a shuttle vehicle. However you ride it, Barr Trail is one tough cookie, with more than 7,000 feet in altitude change! Try to enjoy the spectacular views while struggling to take in the ever-decreasing oxygen. Watch out for other travelers on this busy trail! The National Forest Service may close this trail to bikes due to Kamikaze downhill action. Barr Trail is too crowded for such riding. Add a bell to your bike to warn other trail users of your presence. It is illegal to ride on the toll road. You can sometimes buy a downhill ticket for the Cog Railway (space permitting).

Land status: Pike National Forest.

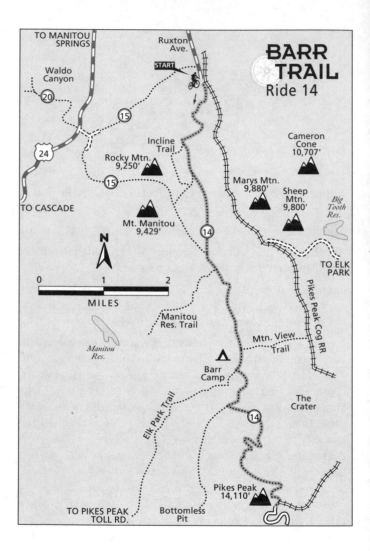

TO MANITOU
SPRINGS

Ruxton
Ave.

START

Waldo
Canyon

**BARR
TRAIL**
Ride 14

20

15

24

TO CASCADE

Incline
Trail

Rocky Mtn.
9,250'

Cameron
Cone
10,707'

15

Marys Mtn.
9,880'

Sheep
Mtn.
9,800'

*Big
Tooth
Res.*

Mt. Manitou
9,429'

14

TO ELK
PARK

N

0   1   2

MILES

*Manitou
Res.*

Manitou
Res. Trail

Pikes Peak Cog RR

Mtn. View
Trail

Barr
Camp

The
Crater

Elk Park Trail

14

TO PIKES PEAK
TOLL RD.

Bottomless
Pit

Pikes Peak
14,110'

Maps: Pike National Forest; USGS Manitou Springs, Pikes Peak.

Access: From Manitou Springs follow the signs to the Pikes Peak Cog Railway. Take Ruxton Avenue south from downtown and follow it past the railway's depot. Turn right into the trailhead parking lot. The trail begins on the south side of the lot. Water and restrooms are available at the trailhead.

The Ride

0.0 Start up the switchbacks. These first 3 miles are the toughest.

2.4 The Incline Trail's lower trailhead is on the right.

2.6 The experimental forest and upper Incline Trail pass by on the right. Ride 15 departs from here.

3.2 Stay on the main trail as the Manitou Reservoir Trail disappears to the right.

4.4 The Mountain View turnoff passes on the left and heads to the Cog Railroad. The most level portion of the ride starts here.

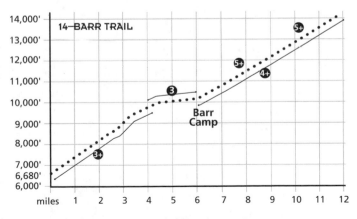

6.0 Barr Camp. Most people turn around here. Heck, camp out in a cabin! The Elk Park Trail heads northwest from here. Those going to the summit continue on the Barr Trail.

7.0 Keep left. The right fork heads to an area called the Bottomless Pit, a Level 4 technical diversion and a good place to turn back for your descent.

8.7 There is a shelter here that should have water. Those riding on should plan on 3 miles of hike-a-bike on very steep, rugged trail.

11.7 Welcome to the summit of Pikes Peak and the view that inspired the words to *America the Beautiful*.

Barr-Ute Trail Loop

Location: Manitou Springs.

Distance: 8.8-mile loop.

Time: 1.5 to 2 hours.

Tread: 5.3 miles of singletrack, 3 miles of dirt road, and 0.5 mile of paved road.

Aerobic level: Strenuous.

Technical difficulty: 4-. Watch for heavily eroded sections on the downhill portion.

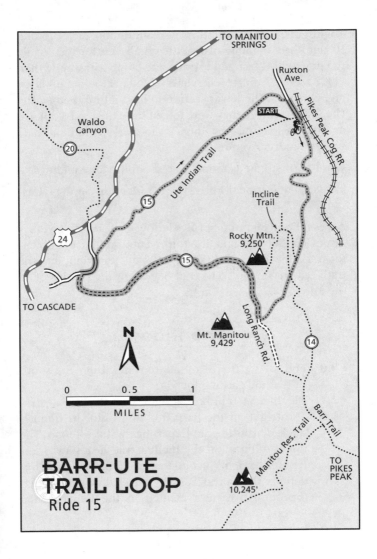

TO MANITOU
SPRINGS

Ruxton Ave.

START

Pikes Peak Cog RR

Waldo
Canyon

20

Ute Indian Trail

Incline
Trail

15

Rocky Mtn.
9,250'

24

15

Long Ranch Rd.

TO CASCADE

14

Mt. Manitou
9,429'

N

0   0.5   1
MILES

Manitou Res Trail

Barr Trail

TO
PIKES
PEAK

10,245'

BARR-UTE
TRAIL LOOP
Ride 15

Highlights: The downhill on the old doubletrack of Long Ranch Road arguably makes the climb worthwhile. While the downhill is fast and furious, the climb gains more than 2,000 feet in 3 miles! The views of Pikes Peak are up close and personal. The lower section follows a trail used by the Ute Indians before they were forced from the land. Look for a singletrack route past the 7-mile mark for an alternate way to Ruxton Avenue.

Land status: Pike National Forest and private holdings.

Maps: Pike National Forest; USGS Manitou Springs, Cascade.

Access: From Manitou Springs follow the signs to the Pikes Peak Cog Railway. Take Ruxton Avenue south from downtown. Follow it past the railway's depot. Turn right into the trailhead parking lot. The trail begins on the south side of the lot.

The Ride

0.0 Follow the Barr Trail as it climbs from the south side of the parking lot.

2.4 The Incline Trail breaks right; stay left.

2.6 Turn right off the Barr Trail and onto the doubletrack. This is the old Experimental Forest road. The upper trailhead of the Incline Trail heads away farther to the right. Just up the road are some old foundations the Forest Service used when monitoring the nonnative trees planted in the Experimental Forest.

3.0 Keep right and climb or push up the eroded road.

3.1 Turn right onto Long Ranch Road.

3.5 Start the downhill!

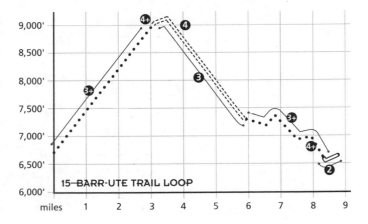

15—BARR-UTE TRAIL LOOP

5.8 Turn right on the dirt road. Then take the next right less than 0.1 mile down the hill.

6.6 The power lines now follow the road.

7.9 Pass by the filtration plant and head down into Manitou Springs.

8.3 Turn right onto Ruxton Avenue and return to the trailhead.

8.8 Trailhead.

16

Ute Valley Park

Location: In Colorado Springs, off Vindicator Road.

Distance: 2.5-mile loop with a variety of other loop options.

Time: 30 minutes. Loop options expand the saddle time.

Tread: 2.5 miles of dirt singletrack. A section of sandstone "slickrock" can be found in this park.

Aerobic level: Moderate. The hill directly behind the school is strenuous but short.

Technical difficulty: 3+. The slickrock, switchback staircase rates a 4+ going down and a 5 going up.

Highlights: Thankfully, the city has saved places like this from development. While not as big as Palmer Park, there is plenty of fun to be had here. The trails run on either side of a ravine making the riding either uphill or downhill, no level terrain. The park has no facilities other than sweet singletrack, ridable rock, and a pond with a boardwalk around it. If your house is near this park, you may find yourself living in this park.

Land status: City of Colorado Springs.

Maps: USGS Pikeview.

Access: From the south take I–25 north, exit at Rockrimmon Boulevard (Exit 147), and follow the exit road around, keeping right at the intersection with Mark Dabling Boulevard. Pass under I–25 and take the next left onto Rockrimmon Boulevard. After 1.5 miles, turn left

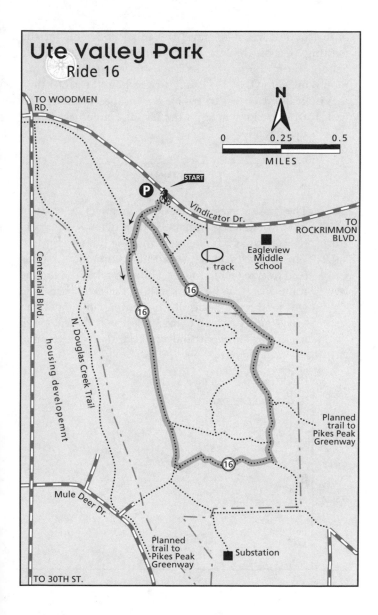

Ute Valley Park
Ride 16

N

| 0 | 0.25 | 0.5 |

MILES

TO WOODMEN
RD.

P START

Vindicator Dr.

TO
ROCKRIMMON
BLVD.

track

Eagleview
Middle
School

16

16

Centennial Blvd.

N. Douglas Creek Trail

housing developemnt

16

Planned
trail to
Pikes Peak
Greenway

Mule Deer Dr.

Planned
trail to
Pikes Peak
Greenway

Substation

TO 30TH ST.

onto Vindicator Drive, travel 0.9 mile, and look for the parking area on the left, 0.2 mile past Eagleview Middle School. From the north take I–25 south, exit at Rockrimmon Boulevard (Exit 147), and turn right and travel 1 mile to Vindicator Drive. Turn right, go another 0.9 mile and look for the parking area on the left, 0.2 mile past Eagleview Middle School.

The Ride

0.0 The trail leaves the parking area via a wooden boardwalk. Keep right and drop down into the park.
0.1 Keep right as a trail enters from the hill to your left.
0.2 This is the main decision time. A number of trails feed to three main routes. This ride takes the middle route that stays to the south of the creek bed. The left-hand route heads down the riparian habitat and leaves either a steep climb back or a technical climb back. The far righthand route heads to Centennial

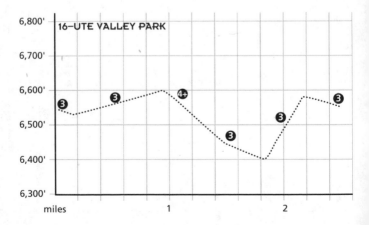

Boulevard and Foothills Trail. Again, we stay to the south (right) of the creek on the middle route.

0.9 After ascending an old, rugged doubletrack, a trail heads off to the left. This ride stays right.

1.1 Turn left here. Straight heads out of the park to Pinion Park and the North Douglas Creek Trail.

1.5 Turn left and head north. The trail to the right heads out of the park.

1.6 Keep right as the trail from mile 0.9 enters from the left.

1.7 Keep left. The trail to the right heads out of the park.

1.8 Keep right as a connector trail enters from the left. It leads to the trail from mile 0.2.

1.9 Turn left and climb. The trail to the right heads out of the park.

2.2 Top of the climb. The trail now descends to the pond.

2.5 Parking lot.

17

Palmer Park

Location: The heart of Colorado Springs.

Distance: Varies. Palmer Park holds more than 25 miles of trails!

Time: As much as you can spare.

Tread: Sweet singletrack. The tread can get soft and sandy during dry spells.

Aerobic level: Easy, moderate, or strenuous. You choose.

Technical difficulty: 3 (beginner), 4 (intermediate), or 5 (expert). You choose. The trails follow the ski-area rating system. Trails marked with a green circle are labeled "beginner." Blue squares are "intermediate," and black diamonds mark "advanced" trails. For our purposes green trails range from 2 to 3, blue are 3 to 4, and black trails warrant a 5 rating.

Highlights: Palmer Park is a mountain biking oasis. This slice of singletrack heaven is surrounded by the entire mass of humanity that is Colorado Springs. If you were going to train an elite force of mountain bikers, you could do the entire program here. Easy rolling trails, rim-wrecking drop-offs, steep climbs over step-like rocks, balance-beam boulders—you name it and Palmer Park has it. Including crowds when the weather is nice. These include hikers, other bikers, and equestrian enthusiasts. Don't forget to yield to all. Why? Because we are having so much fun that we should be in the mood to share our joy and pull over for

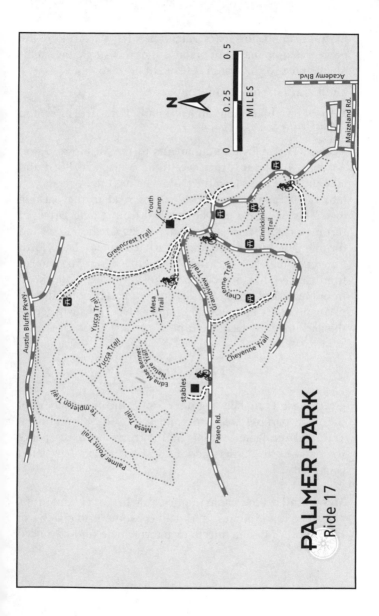

PALMER PARK
Ride 17

the hikers and horseback riders. Besides, if you don't the powers that be may shut bikers out of this singletrack temple. Be nice so the rest of us can continue to enjoy!

Land status: The city of Colorado Springs.

Maps: Local bike shops all have maps of this treasure. Stop in and ask for a free copy.

Access: The main parking area is in the Meadows. From Academy Boulevard, turn west onto Maizeland Road and take the next right into the park. The next right sends you into the Meadows area. Follow this road to the parking lots. This area also can be reached from Circle Drive by turning east on Maizeland Road, passing Chelton Road and turning left into the Palmer Park entrance. The North Canyon Trailhead is reached by taking Paseo Road north from Circle Drive or by turning north onto Chelton Road from Maizeland Road. A lesser-known parking area lies off of Austin Bluffs Parkway on Brenner Place. This will access the park near the Lazy Land picnic area.

The Trails

Greencrest Trail This beginner trail is the only trail out of the main parking area and connects to the Kinnikinnick Trail and the Palmer Point Trail. It runs along the park's west and north borders and ends at the urban Templeton Gap Trail.

Mesa Trail As the name implies, this beginner route runs along the top of a mesa and delivers some prime views of Pikes Peak. Mesa connects to intermediate and advanced trails.

Grandview Trail Another beginner trail that serves up views of distant beauty. From the North Canyon Trailhead, it follows the gentlest grade available to reach a point of quite large vistas. The Cheyenne and Kinnickinnick Trails connect to the Grandview Trail.

Cheyenne Trail Aptly rated "black" and "blue", Cheyenne rides like a roller coaster. The suspension-challenged may find the route a bit jarring at times, while those on heavy steeds may curse the grinding climb up from Paseo Road.

Kinnickinnick Trail The closest intermediate trail to the main parking area, Kinnickinnick makes a serpentine path through its portion of the park serving up tight twists and turns. It's easy to get disoriented on this one. Kinnickinnick connects to the Grandview, Cheyenne, and Greencrest Trails.

Palmer Point Trail A mostly intermediate trail, Palmer Point circles around the northern realms of the park, minus a small section in the south. With connections to the Greencrest, Grandview, Cheyenne, and Edna Mae Bennet Trails, you'll get to know this trail well.

Yucca Trail This intermediate trail provides variety from the Mesa Trail to which it connects. It also provides relief from the Templeton and Edna Mae Bennet Trails if you find you've bitten off more than you'd care to chew.

Edna Mae Bennet Nature Trail Don't let the name fool you into thinking this is a walk in the park. If you don't keep focused, this Level 5 run will give you an over-the-bars look at the earth's surface. Edna connects to the Templeton, Yucca, and Mesa Trails from its terminus at the North Canyon Trailhead.

Templeton Trail This is the sinister cousin of the Mesa Trail. This advanced route loops the rocky, cliff-like portion of the park's northern half. A good place to avoid the crowds. Also a good way to be thrown from your bike. Tight switchbacks with big drops. Sweet.

18

Falcon Trail

Location: United States Air Force Academy.

Distance: 10.9-mile loop.

Time: 2 hours.

Tread: 10.9 miles of singletrack and doubletrack.

Aerobic level: Moderate. While fairly level, the few steeps and obstacles justify the rating.

Technical difficulty: 4. Some riders may have to carry their bikes in a couple of spots.

Highlights: Take a look at what your tax dollars can make! The United States Air Force Academy is a beautiful installation and the Falcon Trail shows it off. It is well signed, with little white falcons, and offers diverse terrain. Odds are pretty good you'll see some of the local mule deer population. The map from the Visitor Center lists the sites, including the fascinating old pioneer home. Don't wander off the trail. Remember, this is a military base! Note: This trail is subject to closure due to fluctuating states of military alert.

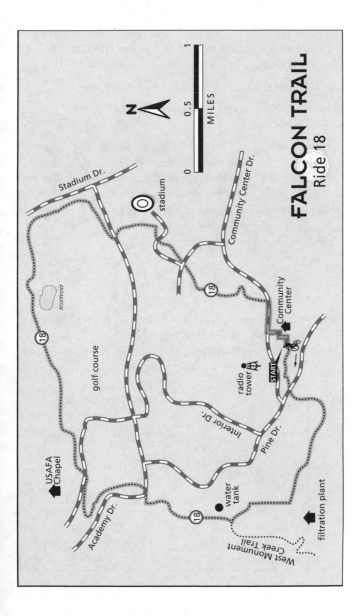

FALCON TRAIL
Ride 18

Standard hours for visitors are 6:30 A.M. to 8:00 P.M. All riders must wear helmets and carry a photo ID with them. All vehicles are subject to search.

Land status: United States Air Force Academy.

Maps: USAFA map (available in the Visitor Center, 719–333–2025); USGS Cascade, Palmer Lake.

Access: Enter the Academy via the south gate, about 9 miles north of Colorado Springs on I–25. After about 2 miles, turn left onto Pine Drive. Go another 3.5 miles and turn right onto Community Drive. After 1 more mile, turn right. Parking is available at the Community Center. The trail starts in the rear right corner (southwest) of the complex and is marked with a big blue sign.

The Ride

0.0 The trail is immediately technical. A portage here is nothing to be ashamed of.

0.5 Cross Pine Drive and then the creek. Keep following the sign of the falcon.

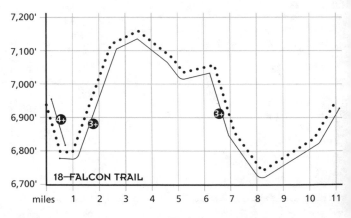

18–FALCON TRAIL

2.4 Keep right as the West Monument Creek Trail intersects on the left.

3.5 Look before crossing Academy Drive!

4.7 Cross Interior Drive.

5.2 Another road crossing. This one is Cross Drive. Gear down for an upcoming steep section.

6.3 Pass the reservoir.

8.1 Academy Drive. The USAFA football stadium is just ahead.

10.0 The trail enters the Community Center complex. Do you remember where you parked?

10.8 The loop is completed.

New Santa Fe Trail

Location: From Colorado Spings to Palmer Lake.

Distance: 17 miles one way. Many trailheads make a variety of distances possible.

Time: 3 hours round trip. New riders may want to plan on a full day and possibly a shuttle vehicle.

Tread: 17 miles of wide, gravel trail in excellent shape.

Aerobic level: Easy. The gradient is gentle enough for trains. The distance ridden can make this rating range from easy to strenuous, depending on fitness level.

Technical difficulty: 2. This is a wide packed gravel trail. However, the pea gravel can make sudden turns slick.

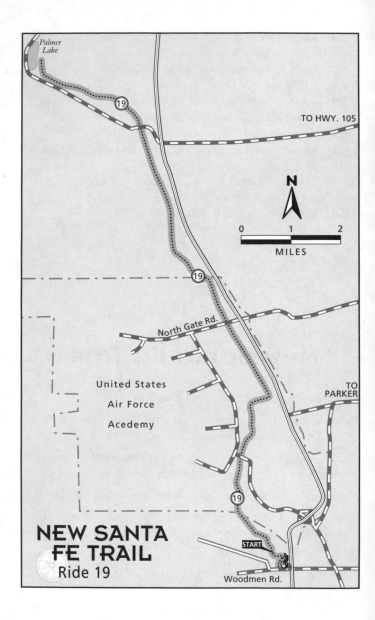

Palmer
Lake

19

TO HWY. 105

N

0   1   2
MILES

19

North Gate Rd.

United States
Air Force
Acedemy

TO
PARKER

19

START

NEW SANTA
FE TRAIL
Ride 19

Woodmen Rd.

Highlights: A long, gentle pedal from Colorado Springs, through the U.S. Air Force Academy to Palmer Lake along an old rail route. Not much in the way of obstacles. A good stroll of a ride in the shadow of Pikes Peak. While on the USAFA grounds, riders must carry a photo ID and wear helmets. Keep in mind this is a busy trail with lots of different user groups.

Land status: Federal, county, and private holdings.

Maps: USGS Palmer Lake, Monument, Pikeview.

Access: The Edmondson trailhead marks the southern end of the trail. Take I–25, exit at Woodmen Road (Exit 149) and head west toward the mountains. The trailhead is 0.25 mile up on the right after crossing Monument Creek.

The middle part of the route, through the USAFA, is open from 6:30 A.M. to 8:00 P.M. Keep in mind that changing degrees of military alert can alter access at any time. To reach the North Gate trailhead, take Exit 156 from I–25 and head west toward the mountains. The trailhead is on the left 0.25 mile from I–25.

The northern terminus of the trail is at the Palmer Lake trailhead. From I–25 take Exit 161 and turn west

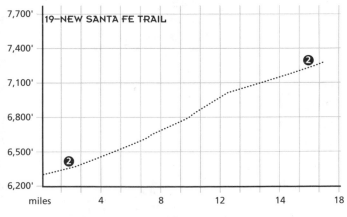

toward the mountains on State Highway 105. Follow Highway 105 through town and on through the town of Palmer Lake. Pass by the lake and turn right onto County Line Road. Cross the railroad tracks and look for the trailhead on the right.

The Ride

0.0 Edmondson Trailhead. Head north up the New Santa Fe Trail. The Pikes Peak Greenway leads away to the south (see ride 24).
2.4 Ice Lake Trailhead.
7.6 North Gate Trailhead.
10.2 Baptist Road Trailhead (Exit 158 off of I–25).
12.9 Monument Trailhead.
17.0 Palmer Lake Trailhead.

20

Waldo Canyon

Location: 2 miles west of Manitou Springs on U.S. 24.

Distance: 7.5-mile loop.

Time: 1.5 to 2 hours, depending on traffic.

Tread: 7.5 miles of hard-packed singletrack with some granite gravel sprinkled on top.

Aerobic level: Moderate.

Technical difficulty: 3+. Tight switchbacks, stretches of root-strewn tread, and granite wheel-grabbers add spice to Waldo.

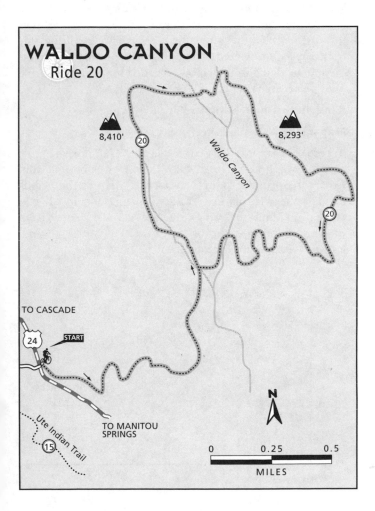

WALDO CANYON
Ride 20

8,410'

8,293'

Waldo Canyon

20

20

20

TO CASCADE

24 START

Ute Indian Trail

15

TO MANITOU SPRINGS

N

0   0.25   0.5

MILES

Highlights: Views of Pikes Peak and Waldo Canyon and pedaling through an established forest with lichen-draped trees and moss-covered rocks make nice distractions. But Waldo is a popular guy and other traffic WILL be on the trail. Some unofficial side trails exist, but this route follows the main, well-worn singletrack. The days of riding this trail may be numbered. There have been numerous right-of-way incidents in which bikers failed to yield. Don't ride here if you aren't prepared to ride socially.

Land status: Pike National Forest.

Maps: Pike National Forest; USGS Cascade.

Access: The trailhead is by the side of U.S. Highway 24 just west of Manitou Springs. Take U.S. 24 westbound from Colorado Springs. About 3 miles past Cave of the Winds Road is the well-marked Waldo Trail parking lot. If you come from Manitou Springs, the lot is about 1.5 miles from the westbound on-ramp of U.S. 24. Carry your bike up a long set of stairs to reach the trail.

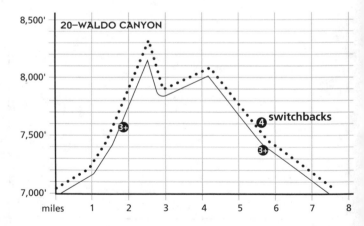

The Ride

0.0 The trail proper starts up the stairs at the registration box. The odometer readings start from here.

0.3 Stay left. A trail goes right about 30 feet to some Pikes Peak granite.

0.9 Stay on the main trail. The small trail to the right overlooks Fountain Creek.

1.7 Take the left fork and climb hard along the stream.

2.5 Turn right at this T intersection. Just a bit farther to the downhill and switchbacks.

5.5 Hang on for a set of tight, twisty switchbacks.

5.8 Back at the fork. Keep left to head home.

Stick a fork in it. It's done! Carry your bike down the steps.

Black Forest Regional Park

Location: North of Colorado Springs in Black Forest.

Distance: There are a number of possible distances with the loop design of the park's trails.

Time: From 15 to 30 minutes. However, the beauty of the park is the loop possibilities. Make up different loops and ride for as long as you like.

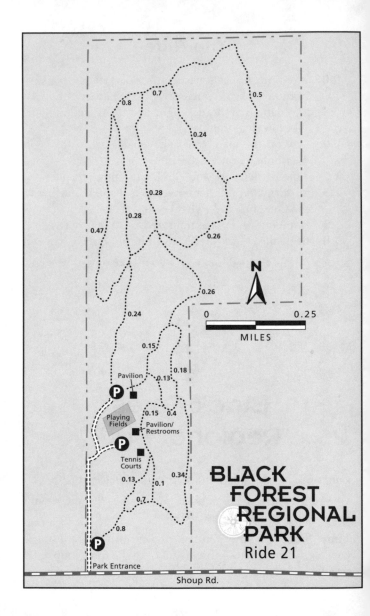

Tread: 3.5 miles of gravel and dirt trail.

Aerobic level: Easy. The hills are short with a moderate grade.

Technical difficulty: 2+. Loose gravel can be tricky.

Highlights: Listen to the sound of the wind through the dark-barked pines as you ride on the easily navigated gravel and dirt trails lit by tree-filtered daylight. A perfectly pleasant pedal. Being neither long nor technically difficult, Black Forest is a good place to practice your skills before taking on more difficult trails.

Land status: El Paso County Park. Call (719)520–6375.

Maps: USGS Black Forest.

Access: From Colorado Springs take I–25 north to Exit 153 (Interquest Parkway). Remain on this road as it joins State Highway 83 north and bends to the left; 3 miles from I–25, turn right onto Shoup Road. Continue 2.2 miles and turn left into the signed park entrance.

The Ride

0.0   Unload your steed and head into the forest. It's next to impossible to get lost. The map shows the mileages of the individual segments for you to make up your own route as you explore the park.

Fox Run Regional Park

Location: North of Colorado Springs in Black Forest.

Distance: 3.2 miles as described.

Time: 20 minutes per loop.

Tread: Miles of 4-foot-wide trail coated with granite gravel. Some gravel slush lies in wait at the base of the hills.

Aerobic level: Moderate. The hill north of the lake is Strenuous but short. The north loop is the easier loop.

Technical difficulty: 3. The trail is wide. However, the granite gravel can cause your front wheel to slip away.

Highlights: Weaving through Ponderosa pines, this trail is an exhilarating ride through the forest. The park has two loops with different characteristics that complement each other well. The trails are pretty short, which allows you to tailor your ride to fit your aerobic ability. The lower loop has steeper climbs and drops on a narrower trail, while the northern loop has an open, casual feel. Look for the small, interpretive signs to rest and learn. Bike-riding isn't welcome around the ponds. The park's restrooms have running water.

Land status: El Paso County Park. Call (719) 520–6375.

Maps: Most of the intersections here post permanent trail maps.

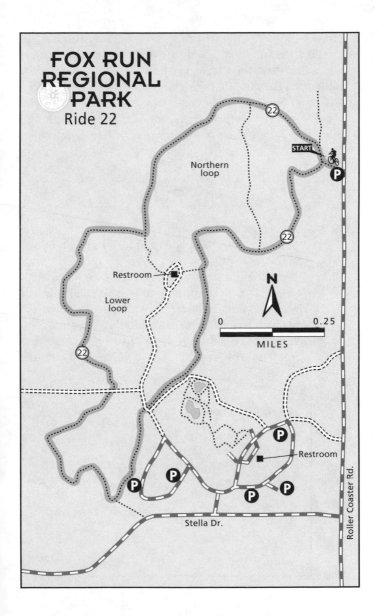

FOX RUN REGIONAL PARK
Ride 22

Northern loop

Lower loop

Restroom

START

P

22

22

22

N

0   0.25
MILES

Restroom

P

P

P

P

P

Stella Dr.

Roller Coaster Rd.

Access: From Colorado Springs take I–25 northbound to Exit 158 (Baptist Road) and turn right. Continue east for 3.4 miles, then turn right on Roller Coaster Road. The trailhead is 0.2 mile on the right. The main entrance to the park is off Stella Road, 0.6 mile past this trailhead. It's also possible to reach the park by exiting I–25 at Glen Eagle and following North Gate Road, making a left onto Roller Coaster Road.

The Ride

0.0 Starting from the trailhead along Roller Coaster Road, head into the woods and turn right after passing by the restrooms.

0.1 Keep left as an unofficial trail leaves to the right.

0.2 A fork! This description continues straight on the right-hand trail. To bisect the northern loop, turn left. This park has maps at every official intersection.

0.7 Keep right. A left here heads to another trailhead complete with restroom. It also connects to the

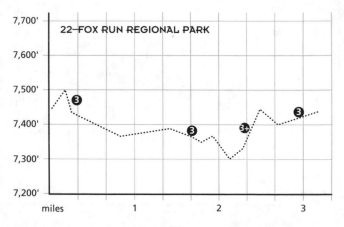

backside of the northern loop (another 0.7 mile back to the start).

1.5 Look both ways and cross over this dirt road.

2.1 The trail dumps into a dirt road. Look across the road for the trail as it climbs beside another dirt road. Yup, that's the route.

2.2 Turn left and head up the steepest part of the ride. A right turn heads to the ponds, where biking is not allowed.

2.5 Keep right. A left turn leads to the restrooms mentioned at mile 0.7.

2.8 Keep right. A left turn leads to the junction at mile 0.2.

3.2 Turn right and pass the restrooms to reach the parking lot. Or stay left and start another loop.

Monument Trail

Location: North of Colorado Springs in Monument.

Distance: 8.5-mile loop.

Time: 1.75 hours.

Tread: 6 miles of singletrack and 2.5 miles of dirt road. The upper portions of dirt singletrack resemble a goat trail and are strewn with embedded rocks. The dirt road is in good shape with some washboards and loose gravel patches.

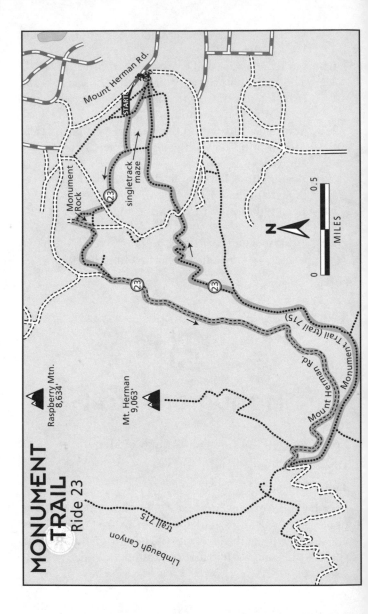

MONUMENT TRAIL
Ride 23

Raspberry Mtn.
8,634'

Mount Herman Rd.

START

Monument Rock

23

singletrack maze

23

23

Mt. Herman
9,063'

Mount Herman Rd.

Monument Trail (trail 715)

Limbaugh Canyon

trail 715

N

MILES

0   0.5

Aerobic level: Moderate. The road is a constant climb. The downhill will have you off the saddle the whole way.

Technical difficulty: 4. The singletrack is extremely narrow and twists up and down rocky sections. The road rates a 2.

Highlights: A maze of singletrack at the trailhead provides lots of loops to play on. Those who journey up the dirt road past Monument Rock are rewarded with views of the plains stretching from the Front Range. Once you get to the highly technical Monument Trail, you won't be able to spare a glance at any view. The oaks will be slapping at your sides and the rock-strewn tread will be grabbing at your wheels. With skill and perhaps some luck, you won't discover why the locals call this "That $*#&in' Trail." The downhill section is currently little more than a goat trail. That's sure to change with use. Please stay on the trail and don't make any shortcuts!

Land status: Pike National Forest.

Maps: USGS Pike National Forest.

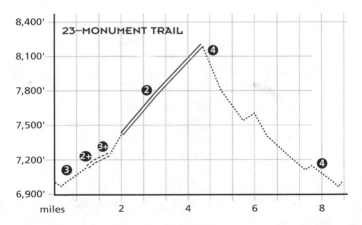

Access: From I–25 in Colorado Springs, head north to Exit 161 and turn left. After crossing over I–25 the road comes to a T intersection with State Highway 105 and the on-ramp to I–25 South. Turn right, and then make the next left onto Third Street, which takes you through Monument. After 0.2 mile you'll cross railroad tracks, then turn left onto Mitchell Avenue. Follow this road south 0.7 mile, then turn right onto Mount Herman Road. Drive 0.6 mile and look for the trailhead's spur road on the left.

The Ride

0.0 Following the trail into the woods from the trailhead sends you into a maze of singletrack that's quite fun. But if you don't like feeling unsure if you're on the right track, just follow Mount Herman Road up to mile 2.0. For those who don't mind wandering the maze, head into the woods at the trailhead and keep right. This description doesn't solve the maze for you. It is definitely a fast and fun place to play.

1.0 Cross the dirt road that heads to the Forest Service fire buildings and head toward Monument Rock. If you made it to this road immediately next to the gate, you'll have to turn left and gain some altitude to reach this route's official road crossing point. If you are south of the Forest Service buildings or right next to them, you need to follow the road northward on its loop then descend a bit to reach this crossing point. When you are at the same altitude as Monument Rock (should be visible to the north) look for the trail.

1.2 Monument Rock. Take time to enjoy the phallic stone and neighboring pond, then find the wide track that heads uphill from the uphill side of Monument Rock. This leads through more pine and oak on the same packed tread.

1.4 A staircase of water bars may slow your progress. Up ahead is a steep pitch with more water bars.

1.9 A four-way intersection. This route turns right toward Mount Herman Road. Left heads to an overlook. Straight heads back toward the maze.

2.0 Mount Herman Road. Turn left and head up the hill.

4.3 Pass by the Mount Herman Trail trailhead at this sweeping hairpin turn and continue up Mount Herman Road.

4.5 The next sweeping left-hand turn is another trail head. The Monument Trail crosses the road here. This ride turns left to enjoy a technical downhill. If you wish to explore further, turn right and head up the trail, and continue into Limbaugh Canyon. There you can loop back to the town of Palmer Lake or connect to the Balanced Rock Road. The old signs call this the Chautauqua Trail. It's now called the Monument Trail. The Forest Service calls it Trail 715.

5.1 The trail is joined by an electrical power line. Turn left, climbing briefly but steeply to keep on this route. If you went straight instead, you'd end up south of Monument. A sign marks the turn.

6.5 Again keep left to reach the final switchback section before recrossing the Forest Service road and re-entering the maze. A right here would send you to a trailhead on Schilling Avenue southwest of this route's trailhead.

7.3 Cross the dirt road and enter into the maze section. Don't worry. Just point the bike down and you'll find the trailhead.

8.5 Trailhead.

Urban Trail System

Location: Throughout Colorado Springs.

Distance: Over 75 miles of trails (150 miles when complete).

Time: Shorter than sitting in rush-hour traffic.

Tread: Urban trail. The main "spine" routes are 12-foot wide concrete and asphalt surfaces with 2- to 4-foot soft shoulders separated by landscaped buffer zone. The city calls these Tier 1 trails. Tier 2 trails (routes that feed into Tier 1 trails) have the same specifications as Tier 1 trails without the landscaping to separate the shoulder from the trail. The system's capillary routes, called Tier 3, tend to have gravel and "natural" surfaces. Tier 3 trails are designed to be 4 to 6 feet wide.

Aerobic level: Easy. The hills that exist are made easier by the hard, wide tread.

Technical difficulty: 1 and 2. The presence of gravel on the Tier 3 trails warrant the 2 rating. Be wary of sudden direction changes on the gravel trails! Your front wheel can slip away from you.

Highlights: Any city that wants to lower its dependence on the automobile and encourage greener ways to get around should look to Colorado Springs for inspiration. This system allows bikers to flow throughout the city on safe, pleasant trails. The main artery of this system is Pikes Peak Greenway (see trail description). Keep in mind these are

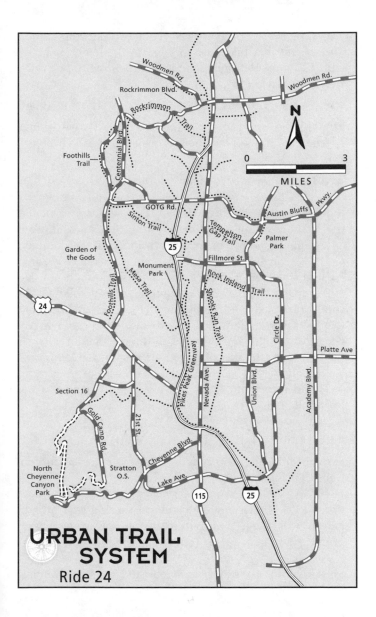

URBAN TRAIL
SYSTEM
Ride 24

shared by every nonmotorized method of moving around known and that bikes are to yield to them all. However, with 12-foot-wide trails there is plenty of room. Just don't ride like a mad dog.

Land status: City of Colorado Springs and private holdings.

Maps: The city government web page (www.springs gov.com) has maps of each trail segment as well as an overview map.

Access: The main advantage of the system is that it is accessible from most neighborhoods. Thus, developed trailheads aren't the focus. If you want to ride a particular trail without riding to it, find a nearby city park and use it as a trailhead. Southern access is available at the Fountain Creek Regional Trail. Northern access is via the New Santa Fe Trail (ride 19). The Greenway's midsection is accessible at Monument Valley Park. From the north follow I–25 southbound, exit on Uintah Street (Exit 143) and turn left (east, away from Pikes Peak). Go 0.2 mile and turn right on Glen Road, following the road to the parking lot. Glen is the first road after crossing the I–25 interchange. From the south, follow I–25 northbound, exit on Uintah Street (Exit 143) and turn right. Go 0.1 mile and turn right on Glen Road following the road to the parking lot.

THE TRAILS (FROM SOUTH TO NORTH):

Several trails are being added to this system. Here are the trails available for riding as of early 2003.

Pikes Peak Greenway 12.4 miles; concrete, asphalt, and gravel. This is the main artery of the system, stretching from the Fountain Creek Trail to the New Santa Fe Trail.

Shooks Run 4.1 miles; concrete and asphalt. Parallels

Nevada Avenue from Fountain Boulevard to the Rock Island Trail. It is slated to connect with the Pikes Peak Greenway.

Midland Trail When completed, this trail will connect the Pikes Peak Greenway with the foothills trail on a route that parallels U.S. 24.

Monument Valley Park 1.0 mile. The Pikes Peak Greenway has a loop here that is popular with the lunch time exersize crowd.

Bear Creek Trail 0.4 mile; gravel. Connects the Pikes Peak Greenway with Bear Creek Regional Park and its trails. This trail is useful to access trails along Gold Camp Road, such as Section 16 (ride 9), the Paul Intemann Trail (rides 10 and 13), and Captain Jack's (ride 1).

Mesa Springs Greenway 3.1 miles; concrete. Provides access to places on the west side of I–25. It connects to the Pikes Peak Greenway in Monument Valley Park. It also provides a route to the Palmer-Mesa and Mesa Valley Trails.

Palmer-Mesa Trail 3.1 miles; asphalt and gravel. Runs from Uintah Street along Mesa Road to connect with the Foothills Trail.

Mesa Valley Trail 3.1 miles; gravel and asphalt. Connects the Mesa Springs Greenway with the middle of the Palmer-Mesa Trail.

Rock Island Trail 4 miles; asphalt. Runs along Constitution Avenue to Academy Boulevard and Homestead Trail near Palmer Park (ride 17).

Sinton Trail 2.8 miles; asphalt and concrete. Brings bikers from the Pikes Peak Greenway to Garden of the Gods Road and the Foothills Trail.

Templeton Gap Trail 4.9 miles; asphalt, gravel, and concrete. Connects to the Pikes Peak Greenway via a gently bending trail. It turns to concrete and asphalt and heads to Union Boulevard, connecting with Greencrest Trail in Palmer Park (ride 17).

Austin Bluffs Trail 2.1 miles; concrete. Follows Austin Bluffs Parkway from Nevada Avenue to the Templeton Gap Trail near Palmer Park (ride 17).

North Douglas Creek Trail 1.3 miles; gravel. Slated to connect the Pikes Peak Greenway to Vindicator Drive and the Foothills Trail, it currently runs along Centennial Boulevard on the west side of Ute Valley Park (ride 16), connecting with Pinon Valley Park.

Rockrimmon Trail 2.5 miles; gravel. Connects the Pikes Peak Greenway to Ute Valley Park (ride 16) and the Foothills Trail.

Foothills Trail 6.2 miles; asphalt and concrete on the southern portions, gravel on the northern reaches. A long trail providing a mostly gravel route between U.S. 24 and Rockrimmon Boulevard. Connects to Palmer-Mesa, Midland, and Woodmen Trails. Access to Garden of the Gods.

Homestead Trail 8.2 miles; varying surfaces. Connects Rock Island Trail with the Cottonwood Creek Trail.

Cottonwood Creek Trail 3.6 miles; gravel. Connects Woodmen Road at Austin Bluffs Parkway to Union Boulevard. It has a short loop through Cottonwood Park.

Skyline Trail 4 miles; concrete. This route runs from Research Parkway past Union Boulevard to the planned Briargate Trail.

Briargate Trail Planned to connect Skyline Trail to Powers Road.

Chamberlain Trail A gravel route planned to reach from Bear Creek Regional Park to points south along Highway 115 and Fort Carson.

Fountain Creek Trail 10 miles; mostly gravel. Extends southward from the Pikes Peak Greenway and meanders along Fountain Creek to Fountain Creek Regional Park. Hike on the park's nature trail for prime bird watching. Take Exit 132 off I–25, then go south 0.5 mile on State Highway 85/87 to the park. This the is southern reach of the Urban Trail System. Someday it may connect through Fort Carson and into Fremont County.

Sand Creek Trail Lots of work to be done on this trail. When completed it will stretch from the southern end of the Pikes Peak Greenway northward along the western portion of the city on a route that passes by Peterson AFB, Powers Boulevard, and Woodmen Road.

Woodland Park–Divide

Woodland Park lies 20 miles west of Colorado Springs on U.S. Highway 24, which continues on into Divide.

Woodland Park offers a full range of services with prices comparable to The Springs. Camping areas are abundant in the surrounding hills. Rampart Reservoir offers three campgrounds and is the setting for ride 25.

Woodland Park also has a couple of bike shops. If you forgot to bring along an extra tube or want to look for a sale on shocks, roll up to the local shop.

The other focal point for visitors to this region is Divide, a small town 7 miles west of Woodland Park. Divide offers very limited services; gas and snacks are available. It is the closest civilization to Mueller State Park.

Mueller State Park has camping available for tents and recreational vehicles. These spots fill up quickly. Call ahead for reservations at (719) 687–2366.

Rampart Reservoir

Location: 10 miles southwest of Woodland Park.

Distance: 14-mile loop.

Time: 2 to 3 hours.

Tread: Excellent conditions throughout the 9.2 miles of singletrack, 3.1 miles of doubletrack, and 1.7 miles of paved road.

Aerobic level: Easy. Some brief climbs, but it's mostly level and long.

Technical difficulty: 3. Smooth singletrack but some tough Level 5 sections can be sought out.

Highlights: This is a good trail to introduce someone to mountain biking. The singletrack dodges around the reservoir among boulders and bushes, and numerous side trails offer endless variety for exploring. While suitable for beginners, gonzo riders won't have to look long for a challenge. Something this inviting does attract crowds, however. The unwritten rule is to ride this route in a clockwise direction—especially on crowded weekends. Whichever way you go, ride in control, which means yielding the right-of-way.

Land status: Rampart Reservoir Recreation Area and Pike National Forest.

Maps: Pike National Forest; USGS Cascade.

Access: From Colorado Springs drive 18 miles west on U.S.

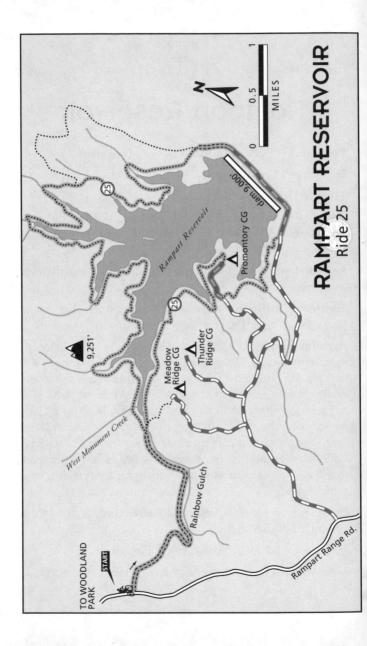

RAMPART RESERVOIR
Ride 25

Highway 24 toward Woodland Park. As you enter the town, turn right just before the McDonald's. Keep straight through the stop signs and past the schools. After 3 miles, turn right at Loy Creek Road and then right again onto Rampart Range Road. Park at the Rainbow Gulch trailhead 3 miles up on the left.

The Ride

0.0 The Rainbow Gulch Trail/Road starts through the gate. Follow this downhill, keeping to the left when the road turns to doubletrack.

1.5 Turn right onto Rampart Reservoir Trail 700 and cross the bridge.

1.6 Keep left at this fork. Right leads to Meadow Ridge Campground. Simply keep toward the shore at all forks.

3.5 Promontory Campground. Ride down the paved road.

3.9 Look for the trail on the left. Take it and return to the lakeshore.

4.7 Paved road again. Turn left and cross the dam.

6.1 The road, now dirt, forks. Turn left onto the single-track.

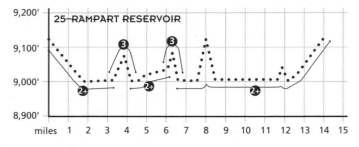

12.5 Turn right at Rainbow Gulch and return to the trail-head.

14.0 Trailhead.

Lovell Gulch

Location: 20 miles west of Colorado Springs in Woodland Park.

Distance: 5.6-mile loop.

Time: 30 to 45 minutes.

Tread: Hard-packed dirt dominates the 4.4 miles of single-track and 1.2 miles of doubletrack.

Aerobic level: Moderate.

Technical difficulty: 3+. A couple of sketchy downhills and an incline laced with roots and rocks warrant the plus rating.

Highlights: The singletrack winds through aspen groves, open meadows, and boulder patches while the doubletrack offers a roller-coaster downhill. Toss in wildflowers or fall colors and a backdrop of Pikes Peak, and the excellent ride recipe is complete. If a pet comes along, please heed the notes at the trailhead.

Land status: Woodland Park Parks and Recreation.

Maps: Pike National Forest; USGS Mount Deception.

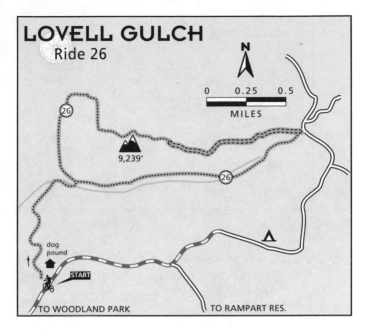

Access: From Colorado Springs drive about 18 miles west on U.S. Highway 24 toward Woodland Park. As you enter the town, turn right just before the McDonald's. Keep straight through the stop signs, past the schools, and bear right. 2.2 miles past the McDonald's, look on the left for the animal shelter. The trailhead shares parking with the shelter.

The Ride

0.0 Cross through the gated entry to the Lovell Trail. Don't forget to close the gate!
0.1 Take the right fork. If nature calls, the left fork has an answer.

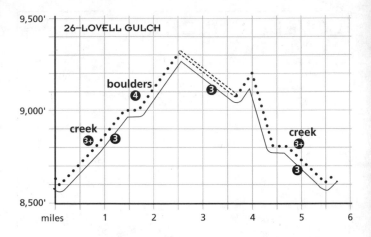

26-LOVELL GULCH

- **0.2** Again, take the right fork and follow the trail markers. The spurs are closed for erosion control. When in doubt, look ahead for the next marker.
- **0.8** Keep some momentum as you cross the creek and turn right onto a doubletrack.
- **1.4** Continue straight ignoring the spur on the left.
- **1.7** Obey the sign and stay on the main trail. Just ahead lies a climb through boulders that may force some ratcheting.
- **2.5** Turn left at the gate. DO NOT go down the graded road. The route heads down the hill beneath the electrical wires.
- **3.7** Keep right as the doubletrack becomes faint.
- **4.0** Turn right. Keep an eye out for the trail marker while speeding down. Again, the markers blaze through confusion caused by erosion.
- **4.4** Left, over the fallen tree.
- **4.7** Turn right and retrace the trail.
- **5.6** Trailhead.

27

Geer Pond Loop

Location: Mueller State Park.

Distance: 10.1-mile loop.

Time: 2 hours.

Tread: 9.8 miles of single and doubletrack; 0.3 mile of paved road.

Aerobic level: Moderate.

Technical difficulty: 3.

Highlights: $5.00 buys a full day of pleasure on this playground's single- and doubletrack. Ride through huge rock outcroppings, open meadows, tranquil ponds, and huge aspen. It's spectacular in the fall as crowds dwindle and leaves change. Occasional trail closures are updated on maps available at the park entrance and everything is well marked. The map for this ride shows other trails open to bikes.

Land status: Mueller State Park.

Maps: Mueller State Park recreational trails; USGS Divide.

Access: From Colorado Springs drive 25 miles west on U.S. Highway 24 to Divide. Turn left at the light onto State Highway 67. Mueller State Park is 4 miles ahead on the right. Turn right and pay $5.00 at the entrance station. Continue down Wapiti Road to the Lost Pond trailhead and park.

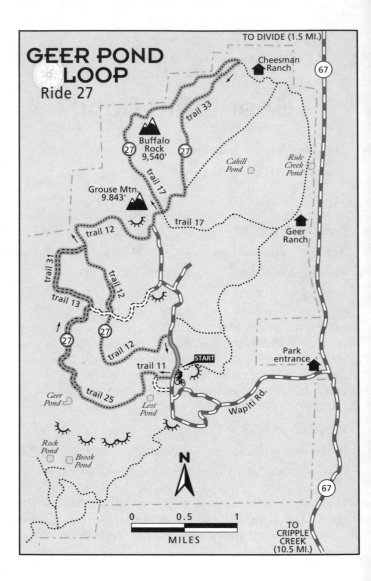

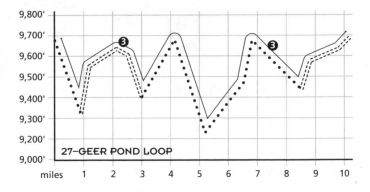

9,800'
9,700'
9,600'
9,500'
9,400'
9,300'
9,200'
9,000'

27–GEER POND LOOP

miles 1 2 3 4 5 6 7 8 9 10

The Ride

- **0.0** Begin on the Lost Pond Trail 11. The trailhead leaves the parking lot to the west and immediately turns right.
- **0.5** Lost Pond. Pick up Geer Pond Trail 25.
- **0.9** Geer Pond. Take the left fork, staying on Trail 25.
- **2.1** Left on Werley Ranch Trail 13.
- **2.5** Right on Mountain Logger Trail 31.
- **3.0** Turn left on Cummings Cabin Trail 15.
- **4.1** Take Trail 17 left at this popular intersection.
- **5.2** Turn right on Buffalo Rock Trail 33.
- **6.5** At Cahill Pond Trail 34, turn right.
- **6.8** Retrace the route onto Trail 15, continuing straight on 15 where Trail 31 intersects.
- **8.5** Turn right on Homestead Trail 12.
- **8.8** Continue straight on Trail 12 as it crosses Trail 13, which leads to the campground.
- **9.8** Turn right on Wapiti Road.
- **10.1** Turn right into the trailhead parking lot.

The Ranch Loop

Location: Mueller State Park.

Distance: 8.7-mile loop.

Time: 1.5 hours.

Tread: 8.7 miles of singletrack and doubletrack.

Aerobic level: Moderate. The route ends with a climb making it seem more strenuous.

Technical difficulty: 3.

Highlights: More bang for your $5.00 entrance fee. While this route connects to the Geer Pond loop (ride 27), it shows a different side of Mueller State Park. Two old ranches, Cheesman and Geer, give this ride an Old West ambiance. Take a lunch and the map and make a day of it. If you want to limit the climbing, simply ride to Cheesman Ranch and back. This will take out a mile-long climb. Of course, it also takes away a 1.5-mile descent.

Land status: Mueller State Park.

Maps: Mueller State Park recreational trails; USGS Divide.

Access: From Colorado Springs drive 25 miles west on U.S. Highway 24 to Divide. Turn left at the light onto State Highway 67. Mueller State Park is 4 miles ahead on the right. Turn right and pay $5.00 ($10.00–$14.00 to camp) at the entrance station. Continue down Wapiti Road to the Elk Meadow or Peak View trailheads (both on the right) and park.

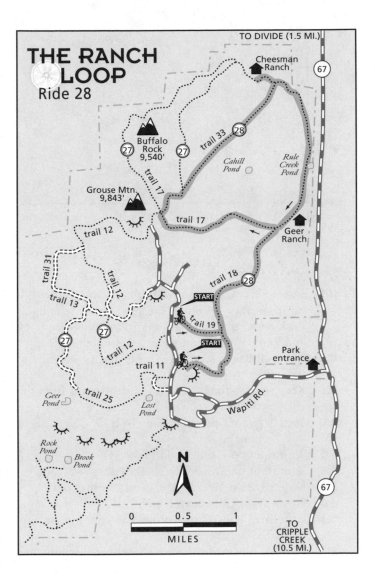

THE RANCH LOOP
Ride 28

TO DIVIDE (1.5 MI.)

Cheesman Ranch

67

Buffalo Rock 9,540'

27

27

trail 33

28

Cahill Pond

Rule Creek Pond

trail 17

Grouse Mtn. 9,843'

trail 17

trail 12

Geer Ranch

trail 31

trail 12

trail 13

trail 18

28

START

trail 19

27

27

trail 12

START

Park entrance

trail 11

Geer Pond

trail 25

Lost Pond

Wapiti Rd.

Rock Pond

Brook Pond

N

67

0   0.5   1

MILES

TO CRIPPLE CREEK (10.5 MI.)

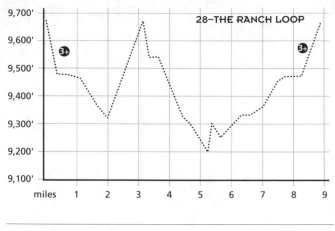

The Ride

0.0 Start at the Elk Meadow Trailhead and follow Elk Meadow Trail 18 down the hill. Those starting at Peak View trailhead will take Peak View Trail 19 and join with this route at the 0.8-mile mark.

0.4 The trail has descended quickly and now bends to the left.

0.8 Keep right as the Peak View Trail 19 enters from the left.

2.0 Turn left on Cheesman Ranch Trail 17 at this T intersection.

3.1 Turn right on Cahill Pond (Trail 34).

3.4 Turn right on Buffalo Rock (Trail 33).

3.6 Keep right on Trail 33 at this fork in the trail.

4.8 Turn left on Cheesman Ranch Trail.

5.1 Cheesman Ranch. Turn around to continue on this route.

5.3 Stay left on Cheesman Ranch Trail at this junction with Buffalo Rock (Trail 33).

6.6 Turn left onto Elk Meadow Trail 18 and retrace the route back to the trailhead.

7.8 Keep left on Elk Meadow Trail where the Peak View Trail joins. You can also head up this trail to the Peak View trailhead and ride the road back to the Elk Meadow trailhead.

8.7 Elk Meadow trailhead.

Raspberry Mountain Trail

Location: South of Divide.

Distance: 5.8 miles out and back

Time: 1 hour.

Tread: 5.8 miles of old doubletrack.

Aerobic level: Moderate.

Technical difficulty: 3+. The plus is for low, overhanging branches and deep, eroded ruts that can surprise a fast-traveling downhiller.

Highlights: Whispering aspens start to raise their voices as the late-summer storms slowly, relentlessly move in. Then the pines join in the forest chorus. Ah . . . Colorado. This ride offers a gradual climb then some roller-coaster hills before a final assault on the mountain. If you don't want to

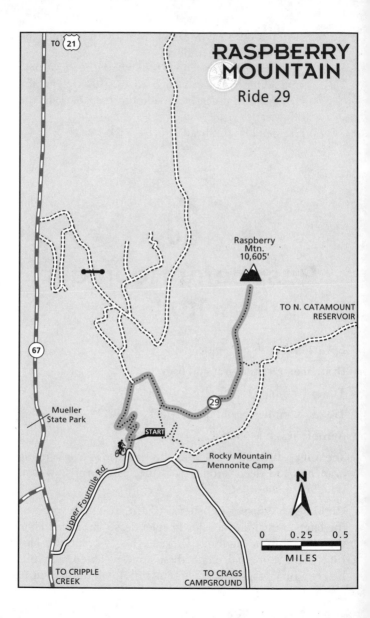

TO 21

RASPBERRY
MOUNTAIN
Ride 29

Raspberry
Mtn.
10,605'

TO N. CATAMOUNT
RESERVOIR

67

Mueller
State Park

29

START

Rocky Mountain
Mennonite Camp

Upper Fourmile Rd.

N

0   0.25   0.5
MILES

TO CRIPPLE
CREEK

TO CRAGS
CAMPGROUND

hike, end the ride at the Granite Fort before the trail takes away all your hard-earned altitude.

Land status: Pike National Forest.

Maps: USGS Divide.

Access: From Colorado Springs drive 25 miles west on U.S. Highway 24 to Divide. Turn left at the light onto State Highway 67. Drive just over 4 miles and turn left on Upper Fourmile Road, a dirt road marked by signs for The Crags Campground and Rocky Mountain Mennonite Camp. The road is rough but passable with caution. Follow the road 1.1 miles to a sharp right-hand hairpin curve. This is the trailhead. Park next to the Forest Service gate and leave room to get by.

The Ride

0.0 Pass the gate that keeps the motorized traffic out and head up the old doubletrack. It quickly begins to switch its way up the hill.

0.5 The climb ends and the trail starts a rise-and-fall pattern.

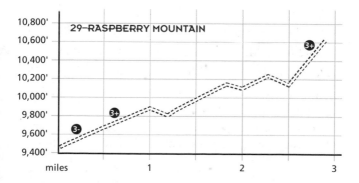

29—RASPBERRY MOUNTAIN

0.9 Keep right here as a power line and a road drop off to the left. From here on out keep left on this main doubletrack.

1.3 Keep left as a ribbon of singletrack leads down to the Rocky Mountain Mennonite Camp and Four-mile Road. Again, keep left for the rest of the way.

2.3 Stay left. The rough road to the right heads down to the access road to North Catamount Reservoir.

2.35 A false summit. The road drops steeply then climbs up the to the top of Raspberry Mountain.

2.9 The real summit.

Horsethief Park

Location: 11 miles south of Divide.

Distance: 4 miles out and back.

Time: 1 hour.

Tread: 4 miles of singletrack with a few rocky patches.

Aerobic level: Moderate. The initial climb is a doozey.

Technical difficulty: 3+. The rocky patches can be tricky.

Highlights: Horse thieves are said to have holed up in the high-country park that is the backdrop of this short gem, which shares a trailhead with ride 31 (Pancake Rocks). Some traces of past occupants still remain. A loop is

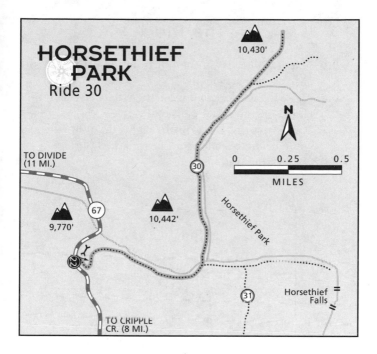

planned for this trail. At press time, however, it wasn't suitable for biking.

Land status: Pike National Forest.

Maps: USGS Cripple Creek North, Pikes Peak.

Access: From Colorado Springs drive 25 miles west on U.S. Highway 24 to Divide. Turn left at the light onto State Highway 67. Pass by Mueller State Park. Eleven miles from Divide, the road passes a closed tunnel. The tunnel's parking area is also the ride's trailhead.

The Ride

0.0 The trail heads up the hill from the southeast corner of the parking area.

0.8 Take the left fork and cross the creek. The right trail leads to Horsethief Falls and ride 23.

1.7 Go left at this fork. To the right, the trail runs 0.5 mile before becoming a cairn-marked portage.

2.0 End of the trail.

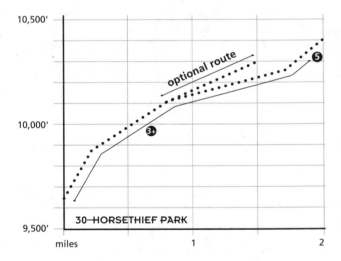

Pancake Rocks

Location: 11 miles south of Divide.

Distance: 5.6 miles out and back.

Time: 1.5 to 2 hours.

Tread: 5.6 miles of singletrack. Roots, tight switchbacks, drop-offs, and erosion show up throughout the ride.

Aerobic level: Strenuous. A lot of climbing in a short distance.

Technical difficulty: 4. The obstacles alone aren't too bad, but pair 'em with the steeps and it's challenging.

Highlights: The Pancake Rocks are just that—rocks that look like pancakes. Getting there is a genuine singletrack challenge through classic mountain terrain. Horsethief Falls is easily accessed and deserves a look.

Land status: Pike National Forest.

Maps: Pike National Forest; USGS Cripple Creek North, Pikes Peak.

Access: From Colorado Springs drive 25 miles west on U.S. Highway 24 to Divide. Turn left at the light onto State Highway 67. Pass by Mueller State Park. Eleven miles from Divide, the road passes a closed tunnel. The tunnel's parking area is the ride's trailhead.

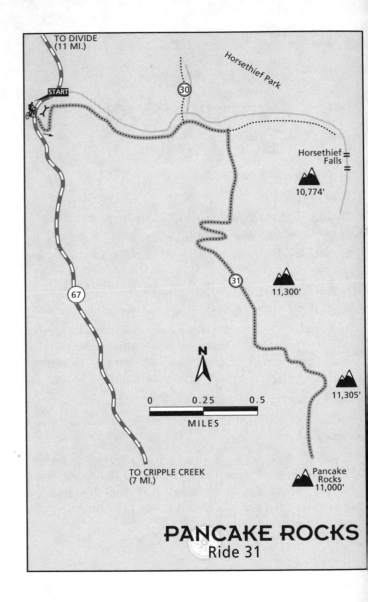

TO DIVIDE
(11 MI.)

Horsethief Park

START

30

Horsethief
Falls

10,774'

67

31

11,300'

N

0   0.25   0.5

MILES

11,305'

TO CRIPPLE CREEK
(7 MI.)

Pancake
Rocks
11,000'

PANCAKE ROCKS
Ride 31

The Ride

0.0 The trail heads up the hill from the southeast corner of the parking area.

0.8 Keep right at the fork. Left is ride 30.

1.0 Turn right. A sign points the way to Pancake Rocks. A left takes you to Horsethief Falls.

1.9 Top of the toughest climb. Contour around the hill to the last climb.

2.8 Pancake Rocks. Retrace the route to return.

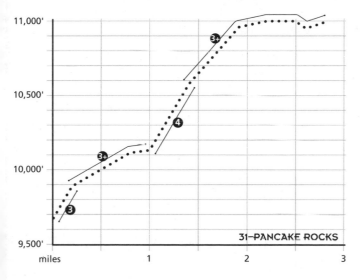

The Crags

Location: 6 miles south of Divide.

Distance: 4.2 miles out and back.

Time: 1 hour.

Tread: 4.2 miles of singletrack. Roots and gravel show up near the end of the trail.

Aerobic level: Moderate.

Technical difficulty: 4. While the beginning of the trail rates a 3, the last stretch gets the 4.

Highlights: Wild rock formations highlight this ride. Views of Pikes Peak and the Catamount reservoirs are also worth the trip. To make a longer and harder ride, start at the highway. An early start may help avoid crowds.

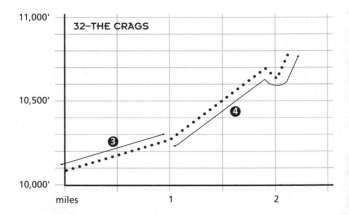

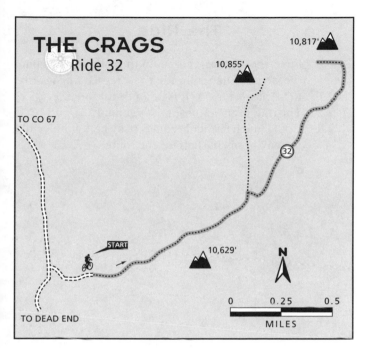

THE CRAGS
Ride 32

10,817'

10,855'

TO CO 67

32

START

10,629'

N

TO DEAD END

| 0 | 0.25 | 0.5 |

MILES

Land status: Pike National Forest.

Maps: Pike National Forest; USGS Pikes Peak, Woodland Park.

Access: From Colorado Springs drive 25 miles west on U.S. Highway 24 to Divide. Turn left at the light onto State Highway 67. Drive just over 4 miles and turn left on a dirt road marked by signs for The Crags Campground and Rocky Mountain Mennonite Camp. The road is rough but passable with caution. Follow the signs to The Crags for 1.5 miles then turn left into the campground. The trailhead is at the end of this road.

The Ride

0.0 From the southeast corner of the parking area climb the steps to the trailhead. The Crags Trail goes left.

1.0 Right at the fork. Left is an optional route.

1.9 The trail bears left before the summit.

2.1 Going much farther becomes risky both to rider and the environment. Retrace the route.

Cañon City

Cañon City (it's pronounced "canyon") lies 45 miles south-west of Colorado Springs. Take State Highway 115 south to Penrose. Turn right onto westbound U.S. Highway 50, which turns into Royal Gorge Boulevard upon entering Cañon City.

To reach Cottonwood Park and the trailhead for rides 35 and 36, turn left from Royal Gorge Boulevard onto Fourth Street. The park is on the right.

Cañon City offers all the amenities of a big city, but with a small-town flavor. The few bike shops are well stocked and have mechanics. Stores tend to close early, however.

Oak Creek Loop

Location: 12 miles south of Cañon City.

Distance: 14.6-mile loop.

Time: 2 hours.

Tread: 2.7 miles of singletrack and 11.9 miles of dirt road.

Aerobic level: Strenuous at first, gaining more than 1,200 feet in the first 2.7 miles. Moderate and mostly downhill from there.

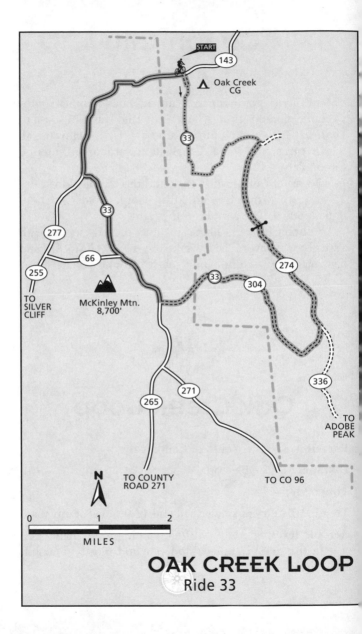

START

143

Oak Creek
CG

33

277

66

33

255

TO
SILVER
CLIFF

McKinley Mtn.
8,700'

274

33

304

271

265

336

TO
ADOBE
PEAK

N

TO COUNTY
ROAD 271

TO CO 96

0   1   2

MILES

OAK CREEK LOOP
Ride 33

Technical difficulty: 3. The singletrack gets narrow with some steep sidehills.

Highlights: This is the best trail in the Cañon City region. This singletrack winds through a narrow, damp ravine among rocks and trees to burst out into a high meadow with a Sangre de Cristo Mountains backdrop. The environment is perfect for wildflowers throughout spring and summer. Descend the roller-coaster-like Forest Road 304 or explore the other connecting roads.

Land status: San Isabel National Forest.

Maps: San Isabel National Forest; USGS Rockvale, Hardscrabble.

Access: From Royal Gorge Boulevard in Cañon City, take Fourth Street across the river and out of town. At about 1.5 miles look for the right-hand turn onto County Road 143. This road turns to a washboarded dirt road. Continue 12 miles and turn left into the Oak Creek Campground. The trailhead is at the end of this road.

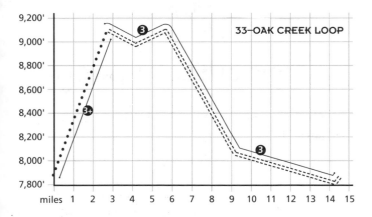

0.0 The trail leaves the parking area from the southwest corner. Spin that granny gear!

2.7 Welcome to the top! Turn right onto FR 274 and cross the meadow. Go through the gate ahead; be sure to close it behind you.

5.7 Turn right onto FR 304 to start the descent. Hang on and remember to keep the rubber side down. The Forest Service map offers some options from here.

9.2 Turn right onto County Road 143. Keep on this main road as it descends the Oak Creek basin.

14.4 Oak Creek Campground. Turn right for one last (brief) climb.

14.6 Back at the beginning.

Tanner-Stultz Loop

Location: 8 miles south of Cañon City.

Distance: 12.1-mile loop.

Time: 2.5 to 3 hours.

Tread: 9 miles of singletrack and 3.1 miles of dirt road. The uphill portion is littered with gravel and rocks and the downhill is like a steep, rock staircase. The climb has been

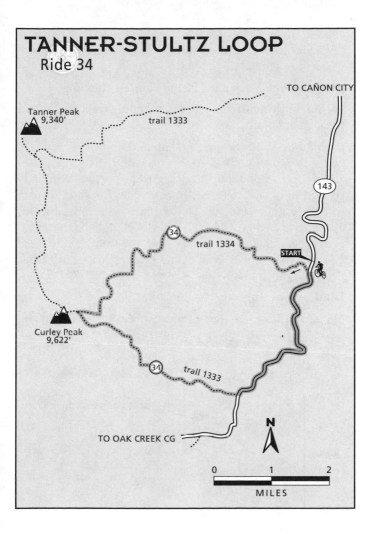

chewed up by ATVs, making it a wide singletrack or a narrow doubletrack. Either way, it is loose and none-too-pleasant to climb.

Aerobic level: Strenuous. Plenty of steep climbing!

Technical difficulty: 5+. The downhill is well-suited for a trials competition.

Highlights: With the gonzo climb to the top, the view had better be worth it. It is. The Sangre de Cristo Mountains and the Wet Mountain Valley spread out below. Wildflowers and hills lined with scrub oak make for good scenery spring, summer, and fall. The aerobic and technical workouts are very intense. Plan on some walking. If you want an even bigger challenge, start at Trail 1333 on County Road 143 and visit Tanner Peak before heading across to Curley Peak and down this route.

Land status: San Isabel National Forest.

Maps: San Isabel National Forest; USGS Rockvale, Curley Peak.

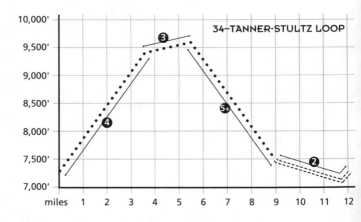

Access: From Royal Gorge Boulevard in Cañon City, take Fourth Street across the river and out of town. At 1.5 miles, just after climbing a hill, look for the right-hand turn onto County Road 143. This road turns to a washboarded dirt road. Continue 6 miles to the trailhead parking on the left. It's marked as Tanner Trail 1334.

The Ride

0.0 Cross County Road 143 and climb onto Tanner Trail 1334. Be ready to climb hard for the first 5.5 miles.

0.9 The trail forks. Either way is workable but the trail on the right is more gradual.

1.3 Take the right-hand trail at this fork for better tread.

2.8 The trail runs up a scree hill.

3.0 Go straight across this intersection.

3.6 Pick a path around the fallen tree.

4.0 The tread improves but it's still uphill.

5.3 A secondary trail cuts left, a shortcut. This route stays right.

5.5 Curley Peak is just ahead. Turn left and head down East Bear Gulch. A sign points to County Road 143. This is Trail 1333.

6.7 The surf is starting to rise! The first obstacle is a fallen tree; boulders, drop-offs, and switchbacks follow.

9.0 Turn left on County Road 143.

12.1 Back to the trailhead.

Grape Creek

Location: Cañon City.

Distance: 18 miles out and back.

Time: 2.5 hours.

Tread: 6 miles of singletrack, 9.4 miles of dirt road, and 2.6 miles of paved road. The singletrack gets pretty rugged. Watch for cactus!

Aerobic level: Moderate.

Technical difficulty: 3+. The road portion of the ride rates a 2.

Highlights: This singletrack wanders along Grape Creek for a good look at an arid canyon and the remains of the old railway to Westcliffe. This trail is open most of the year, but heavy snows or high runoff can shorten the season. Park in Temple Canyon Park to ride just the singletrack. Watch for rattlesnakes and cactus.

Land status: Bureau of Land Management and Temple Canyon Park.

Maps: San Isabel National Forest; USGS Royal Gorge.

Access: This ride begins on the southwest edge of Cañon City. Visitors can park in Cottonwood Park. Reach the park from Royal Gorge Boulevard by crossing the Arkansas River via First or Fourth Street. The park lies between these two streets. To ride only the singletrack, follow ride directions to mile 6.0 and park near the restrooms.

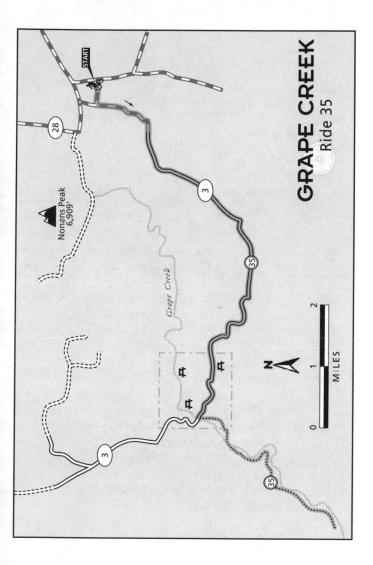

GRAPE CREEK
Ride 35

START

28

3

35

3

35

Nonans Peak
6,909'

Grape Creek

N

MILES
0   1   2

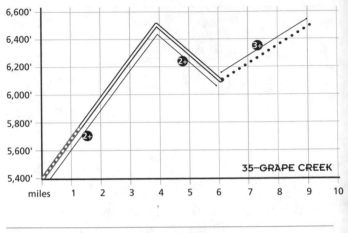

35—GRAPE CREEK

The Ride

0.0 From Cottonwood Park ride west to First Street and turn left.

0.8 Turn right as First Street runs into Temple Canyon Road (County Road 3).

1.3 The road turns to gravel.

6.0 Descending toward the bridge, look to the left for a parking area, directly across from a modern outhouse. This is the entrance to the trail. It isn't well marked but it's easy to find. Crossing the bridge means you've gone too far.

7.0 Drop down to Grape Creek and cross. This can be very tricky (and dangerous) when the water is high. Don't cross if your safety is in doubt.

9.0 End of the line. Retrace the route.

36

Skyline Drive

Location: Cañon City.

Distance: 7.6-mile loop.

Time: 1 hour.

Tread: 7.6 miles of paved road.

Aerobic level: Moderate. The climb is fairly constant for 5 miles.

Technical difficulty: 1. The only difficulties are with vehicular traffic.

Highlights: The bird's eye views of Cañon City and the state penitentiary are grand from this prisoner-built road. This is a good workout with a fun downhill portion. However, it is very exposed both to the sun and cars. Be careful on both accounts.

Land status: Various public and private holdings.

Maps: San Isabel National Forest; Cañon City street map; USGS Royal Gorge, Cañon City.

Access: This ride begins in Cañon City. Park in Cotton-wood Park. From Royal Gorge Boulevard (U.S. 50) you can reach the park by crossing the Arkansas River via First or Fourth Street. Parking is available throughout the park. The odometer readings below begin from the parking lot near the tennis courts.

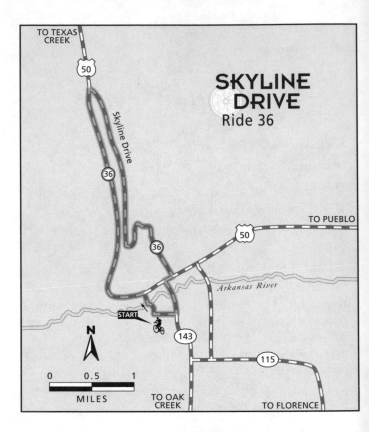

The Ride

0.0 Exit the park by turning right onto Second Street. Then turn left onto Riverside.

0.2 Turn right onto First Street.

0.4 Turn left onto Royal Gorge Boulevard (U.S. 50). Ride on the right shoulder. It narrows around the bend but soon widens.

3.4 Turn right and enter Skyline Drive.

5.5 The top. Now you know why Cañon is pronounced canyon. Enjoy the downhill that follows.

6.1 Turn right onto Fifth Street.

6.8 Turn right on Royal Gorge Boulevard.

7.0 Turn left on Fourth Street.

7.3 Go right on Griffin Avenue and into Cottonwood Park.

7.6 Back at the car.

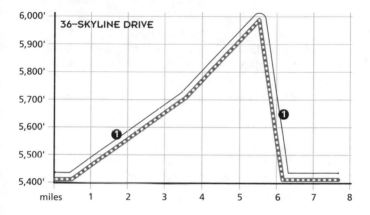

San Isabel Lake

San Isabel Lake is a forty-acre reservoir nestled in the Wet Mountains about 75 miles southwest of Colorado Springs. From Colorado Springs drive 35 miles southwest on State Highway 115 through Penrose and into Florence. Turn left and drive 11 miles south to Wetmore on CO 67. Turn right onto CO 96 and climb up and over Hardscrabble Pass 10 miles to McKenzie Junction. Turn left onto CO 165 and drive 18 miles south to the lake.

San Isabel Lake offers only limited lodging. Camping, however, is fairly plentiful with Ophir Creek, Davenport, and San Isabel campgrounds. Supplies are sparse. It's wise to bring all you'll need with you and gas up the car in Florence.

A unique site in the area is the Bishop Castle. It is on CO 165 about 10 miles north of the lake. Jim Bishop is building the castle by hand. It is free to visit, but he is funding it solely from sightseers' donations.

Snowslide Trail

Location: About 45 miles south of Cañon City; 0.4 mile south of San Isabel Lake.

Distance: 5.2 miles one way.

Time: 1.5 hours.

Tread: 5.2 miles of singletrack.

Aerobic level: Strenuous; steep, but not too long. The elevation graph looks tame, but that's because the scale is in 500-foot increments. This ride has you climbing almost 3,000 feet in about 4 miles!

Technical difficulty: 4. Erosion on the steeps has created some rough going.

Highlights: Views include Pueblo Reservoir, the old Pueblo steel mill, and the Sangre de Cristo Mountains. The challenging singletrack is steep and technical as it winds up through raw and unspoiled forest. Link this trail with the Cisneros Trail (see ride 38) via Greenhorn Mountain Road for a loop with a good downhill run.

Land status: San Isabel National Forest.

Maps: San Isabel National Forest; USGS San Isabel.

Access: From San Isabel Lake drive 0.4 mile south on State Highway 165. The Snowslide Trail sign is on the right. A parking area is on the left.

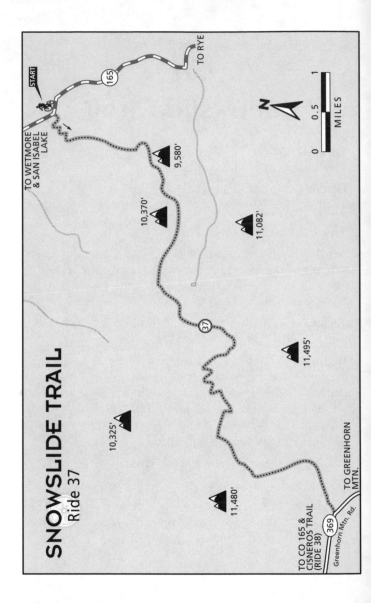

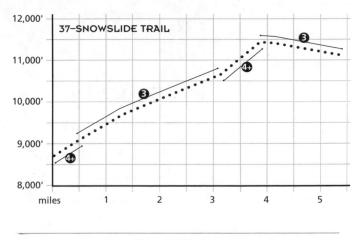

The Ride

0.0 The trail jumps straight into the woods and becomes steep and technical.
0.5 The tread grows smoother and a bit less steep.
3.1 Switchbacks. And you thought it was steep before!
3.8 Finally! The climb ends.
4.0 Start down to the road.
5.2 Greenhorn Road. Turn around and retrace your tracks, or turn right and head for the Cisneros Trail (ride 38).

Cisneros Trail

Location: San Isabel Lake.

Distance: 7.6 miles one way.

Time: 2 hours up and 45 minutes down.

Tread: 5.9 miles of singletrack, 0.5 mile of gravel road, and 1.2 miles of paved road.

Aerobic level: Moderate. The steeps are strenuous but spread out a bit.

Technical difficulty: 3+.

Highlights: The initial granny gear climb gives access to gorgeous meadows and an old mine's spur trail. Snowmobilers use the upper region in the winter. Following their blazes (orange diamonds) will lead you astray. But if you get off track, those same blazes will lead you to Greenhorn Mountain Road, where a left sends you to the upper trailhead. For a loop with the Snowslide Trail (ride 37), the Cisneros Trail is the more gradual climb of the two.

Land status: San Isabel National Forest.

Maps: San Isabel National Forest; USGS San Isabel.

Access: This ride begins at San Isabel Lake. The odometer readings start at the south entrance to the recreational area just past mile marker 19 on State Highway 165. Parking is available 0.2 mile north of the entrance on the highway or in numerous places within the recreational area.

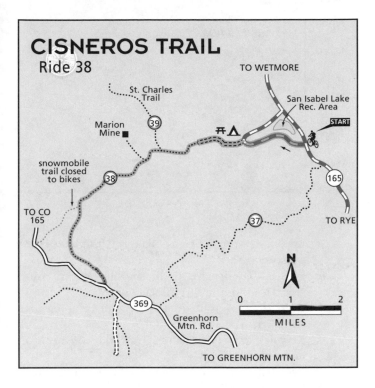

The Ride

0.0 During fall, a gate closes the south entrance of the recreational area to cars. Keep to the main road, avoiding the picnic and camping areas. There is an area map on the right side of the road. This starting point also gives your muscles a warm-up before the real climbing starts.

1.2 As the main road starts to bend right, turn left toward the Cisneros Trail and follow the signs.

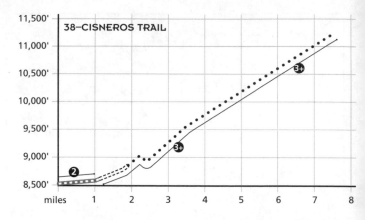

1.7 Keep following the signs; make a left followed by a right.

2.0 This is the Cisneros trailhead with parking available. Head up the singletrack.

2.4 Keep right. A trail from the group camping area joins here.

2.9 Keep left as the St. Charles Trail (ride 39) peels off to the right.

3.4 Keep left. This spur heads to the Marion mine ruins.

5.3 Cross Amethyst Creek.

5.4 Turn left at this fork. Right follows a snowmobile trail to Greenhorn Mountain Road.

5.8 Cross the St. Charles River. No, it doesn't look like a river.

7.6 Greenhorn Mountain Road. Turn around to reap your rewards, or turn left to complete a loop with Snowslide Trail (see ride 37).

St. Charles Peak

Location: San Isabel Lake.

Distance: 15-mile loop.

Time: 3.5 hours.

Tread: 9.6 miles of singletrack and 5.4 miles of paved road. Some swampy conditions may exist around the 5-mile mark and loose gravel shows up on the steeps.

Aerobic level: Strenuous. Steeps in excess of 1,000 feet per mile on this one!

Technical difficulty: 4. Steep, tight switchbacks make for an interesting descent.

Highlights: The feeling of accomplishment is almost as great as the views from St. Chuck. This major-league work-out and technical test is surrounded by beauty on par with the rest of the area. Take your time and enjoy the sights.

Land status: San Isabel National Forest.

Maps: San Isabel National Forest; USGS San Isabel, St. Charles Peak.

Access: This ride begins at San Isabel Lake. The odometer readings start at the south entrance to the recreational area just past mile marker 19 on State Highway 165. Parking is available 0.2 mile north of the entrance on the highway or in numerous places within the recreational area. In the fall, a gate closes the entrance to the recreational area to cars.

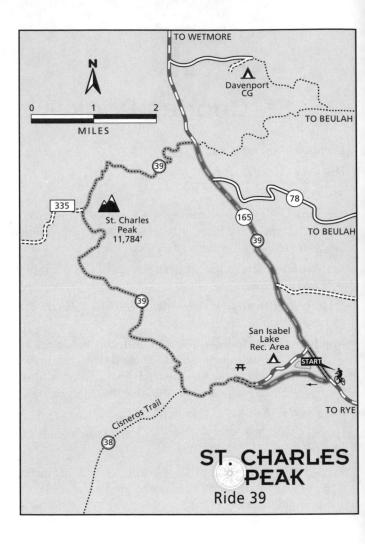

TO WETMORE

N

0   1   2
MILES

Davenport
CG

TO BEULAH

39

335

St. Charles
Peak
11,784'

78

165

39

TO BEULAH

39

San Isabel
Lake
Rec. Area

START

TO RYE

Cisneros Trail

38

ST. CHARLES PEAK
Ride 39

The Ride

0.0 Start at the south entrance to the recreational area. Keep to the main road, avoiding the picnic and camping areas.

1.2 As the main road starts to bend right, turn left toward the Cisneros Trail and follow the signs.

1.7 Keep following the signs; make a left followed by a right.

2.0 This is the Cisneros trailhead with parking available. Head up the singletrack.

2.4 Keep right. A trail from the group camping area joins here.

2.9 Turn right and head up the St. Charles Trail.

4.0 Catch a glimpse of Lake Marion to the left as the climb levels out and the track becomes swampy.

5.6 Keep right as Forest Road 335 intersects the trail. FR 335 leads down to Greenhorn Mountain Road.

6.8 Contour around the summit and begin to head down. Many tight switchbacks lie ahead.

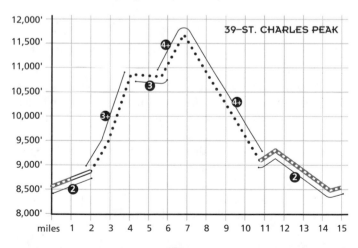

10.8 Turn right on CO 165. A brief climb, then more downhill.

11.5 Keep on the main road as CO 78 joins from the left.

14.4 Pass by San Isabel Lake.

15.0 Back at the beginning.

40

Squirrel Creek

Location: 6 miles north of San Isabel Lake.

Distance: 4.2 miles out and back.

Time: 1 hour.

Tread: 4.2 miles of singletrack.

Aerobic level: Moderate. This is the most gradual of the region's trails and we're pointed downhill all the way.

Technical difficulty: 4. The trail mingles with the creek and a boulder field.

Highlights: This ride offers a fun descent through a variety of creek environments. It starts in an open valley, then twists into a narrow, rocky gorge, and ends above an arid canyon. Technical challenges range from numerous creek crossings to a large boulder field. Keep your eyes peeled for wildlife. I saw a mountain lion in the canyon. The trail can be used as a downhill, a shuttle ride to Beulah, or as a link to the Lion Park Trail. While Lion Park would be a strenuous climb, the downhill is aerobically easy.

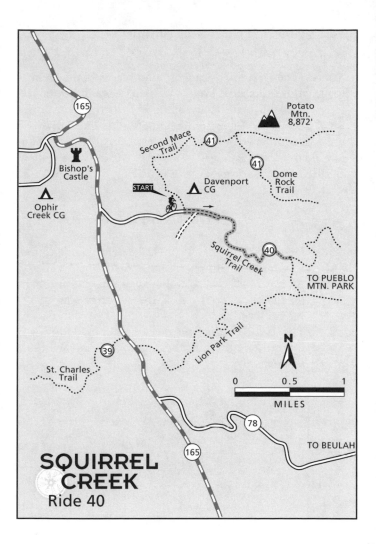

165

Second Mace Trail

41

Potato Mtn. 8,872'

41

Dome Rock Trail

Bishop's Castle

START

Davenport CG

Ophir Creek CG

Squirrel Creek Trail

40

TO PUEBLO MTN. PARK

39

Lion Park Trail

St. Charles Trail

N

0   0.5   1

MILES

78

165

TO BEULAH

SQUIRREL CREEK
Ride 40

Land status: San Isabel National Forest.

Maps: San Isabel National Forest; USGS St. Charles Peak.

Access: The Davenport Campground serves as the launching point for this ride. From San Isabel Lake drive about 6 miles north on State Highway 165. Turn right on Forest Road 382 at the Davenport Campground sign. Drive 1.3 miles down this dirt road. On the left is an old, brick chimney. This is the trailhead. This also makes an excellent shuttle ride by parking a car in Beulah.

The Ride

0.0 Descend FR 382 into the Davenport Campground. Stay on the main campground road.

0.2 As the road sweeps right, keep straight and start down the Squirrel Creek Trail. A large sign marks the trailhead.

0.4 This is the first of nine creek crossings. This one is pretty smooth, but they get progressively more technical.

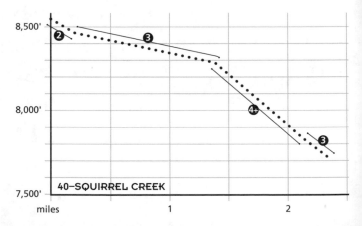

1.4   An old cement wall lies along the creek.

1.6   This boulder field gets a tech rating of 5+. An excellent rider may be able to descend it, but only the superhuman will be able to climb this stretch. Another old wall is a short distance downstream from here.

1.8   This creek crossing can be very slick.

2.0   The trail finally smooths out. A very faint trail to the right leads to Lion Park Trail.

2.1   An old foundation zips by on the right.

2.3   The trail widens, skirting the canyon's rim and an old wooden railing. Turn around before you make the return trip too long. Continuing downhill leads to Pueblo Mountain Park and Beulah.

Second Mace–Dome Rock

Location: 6 miles north of San Isabel Lake.

Distance: 25.7-mile loop.

Time: 5 hours.

Tread: 8.3 miles of singletrack, 12.1 miles of dirt road, and 5.3 miles of paved road.

Aerobic level: Strenuous. It can be shortened to create a moderate ride.

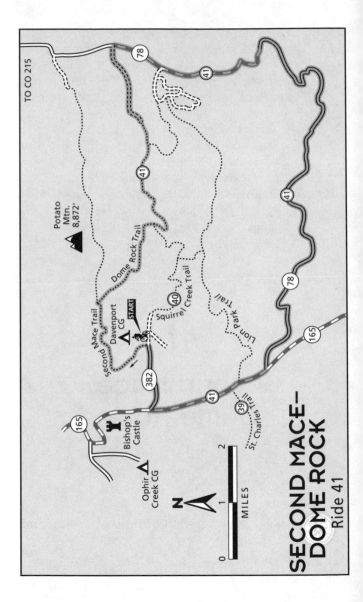

**SECOND MACE–
DOME ROCK**
Ride 41

Technical difficulty: 4+. The trip to Dome Rock rates a 3+ with the main difficulties following.

Highlights: Dome Rock is an impressive blob of rock overlooking a rugged canyon. Some folks may want to turn around after the moderate trip to the rock, rather than tackling the long, technical downhill and 10-mile climb that follows. Use a shuttle to make this terrific all-downhill technical test.

Land status: San Isabel National Forest.

Maps: San Isabel National Forest.

Access: The Davenport Campground serves as the launching point for this ride. From San Isabel Lake drive about 6 miles north on State Highway 165. Turn right on Forest Road 382 at the Davenport Campground sign. Drive 1.3 miles down this dirt road. On the left is an old, brick chimney. This is the trailhead. This also makes an excellent shuttle ride by parking a car in Beulah.

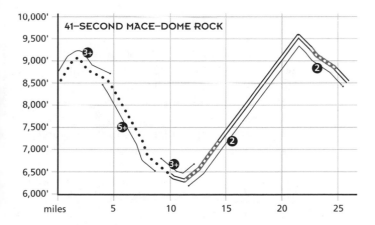

The Ride

0.0   From the chimney, head uphill. The Second Mace Trail starts to the rear left of the little valley. Cross the tiny brook and switchback up the hill to the left.

1.0   Turn right at this T intersection. A broken-up sign labels Beulah as 6 miles downhill and CO 160 as left 1 mile.

1.5   After some rolling terrain, the trail becomes rocky and loose.

1.7   Watch out for a fallen tree here. Up ahead the trail bursts into a beautiful meadow.

2.4   Another T intersection. Turn right to Dome Rock. The left trail continues above Dome Rock and down to Beulah.

4.2   After crossing creek beds a few times, both wet and dry, Dome Rock comes into view. This is where many riders turn around.

4.6   The trail gets a bit confusing after a brief downhill into the woods. A large root and some fallen limbs bar the path ahead. Heed this hint and take the tight left-hand turn.

4.7   The base of Dome Rock. The point of no return.

5.1   The tech level has just risen to a 5. It will continue in the 4-5 category for almost a mile. When confronted with a confusing trail choice, head downstream.

6.1   The creek-crossing frequency is increasing and the crossings are often wet. On the plus side, the trail fattens up.

7.2   After about fourteen creek crossings, the Squirrel Creek Picnic Shelter comes into view. This National Forest Historical Site was one of the Forest Service's first recreational facilities, originally built in 1919.

7.8	After seven more creek crossings, turn left at this trail junction down toward Beulah.
8.3	The trail becomes doubletrack, then a dirt road. Follow this downhill into Beulah.
10.0	Turn right at a four-way intersection. Stay on the main road.
11.1	Turn left at the T junction, then immediately turn right onto Pine Drive (CO 78).
12.3	Stay on CO 78 as it winds up past Pueblo Mountain Park. It turns to dirt after 1 mile and continues on a long, constant climb.
22.2	Turn right onto CO 165.
22.9	Pass by the Lion Park and St. Charles trailheads.
24.4	Turn right down FR 382 and descend toward the Davenport Campground.
25.7	Collapse at the car.

Deer Peak

Location: 8 miles north of San Isabel Lake.

Distance: 18.2-mile loop.

Time: 4 hours.

Tread: 16.1 miles of dirt road and 2.1 miles of extremely rough four-wheel-drive road with boulders a-plenty.

Aerobic level: Strenuous.

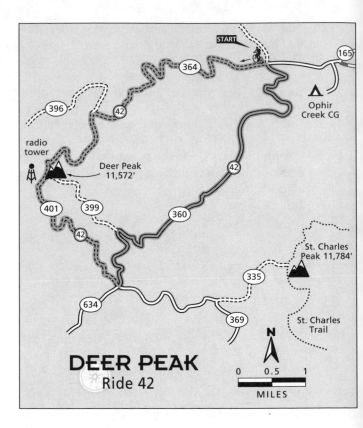

DEER PEAK
Ride 42

0   0.5   1
MILES

N

Technical difficulty: 4. The four-wheel-drive road is boulder-strewn and steep.

Highlights: This is an extreme workout NOT for the faint-hearted! Deer Peak does offer unobstructed views and some wildlife is bound to scamper by during the climb. The last stretch of downhill is through an old mining district. Traces of prospect holes and mines litter the road-side. You may want to reverse the direction and ride the loop clockwise. This puts the climb on better surfaces and makes the downhill steeper and bumpier.

Land status: San Isabel National Forest and private holdings.

Maps: San Isabel National Forest; USGS Deer Peak.

Access: From San Isabel Lake drive 7 miles north on State Highway 165. Turn left at the Ophir Creek Campground sign onto Forest Road 360. Continue over the cattle guard and up the road. At the 0.2-mile point FR 364 peels off to the right. Park and ride.

The Ride

- **0.0** Ride up FR 364 to the east.
- **1.1** Keep straight on the main road.
- **2.4** Bear right onto FR 396.
- **3.1** After passing an old shack, turn left and left again. In other words, keep left through the entire intersection.

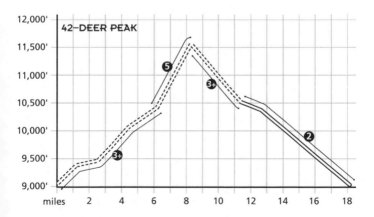

3.4 Two sweeping hairpin corners are due up anytime now.

6.1 Turn left onto FR 401. This road gets very rough as it weaves through a logging area then up Deer Peak. Deer Peak is the one with the towers on it.

8.2 Deer Peak summit. Don't touch the equipment! When ready to leave, continue on FR 401. FR 399 is a rougher descent option from here.

8.7 Keep left each time a road joins this one.

11.3 Turn left onto FR 360. The other road heads to the hamlet of Gardner.

11.9 A tornado once tore through this region. A sign here describes the carnage.

12.5 FR 399 has descended from Deer Peak to join the main road. Stay on FR 360 from here on out. The mining district lies just ahead.

18.2 Right back where it all started.

Junkins Park Loop

Location: 15 miles north of San Isabel Lake and 18 miles east of Westcliffe.

Distance: 17-mile loop.

Time: 2.5 hours.

Tread: 14.8 miles of dirt road and 4 miles of paved road.

Aerobic level: Moderate. The first 9 miles climb gradually.

Technical difficulty: 2.

Highlights: This picturesque ride doesn't require any special technical abilities. The initial ascent parallels a brook that runs amongst boulder outcroppings and aspens. Check out the domesticated elk ranch as the road levels out, then pedal through Junkins Park. The Sangre de Cristo views and rapid descent just add to the fun.

Land status: San Isabel National Forest and private holdings.

Maps: San Isabel National Forest; USGS Hardscrabble, Rosita, Deer Peak.

Access: From San Isabel Lake drive 15 miles north on State Highway 165 to McKenzie Junction and turn left on CO 96. The next left is County Road 358. This is the trailhead. Drive up the road a bit and park. 4 miles up CO 96 is an alternate trailhead where Rosita Road (CR 347) meets the highway.

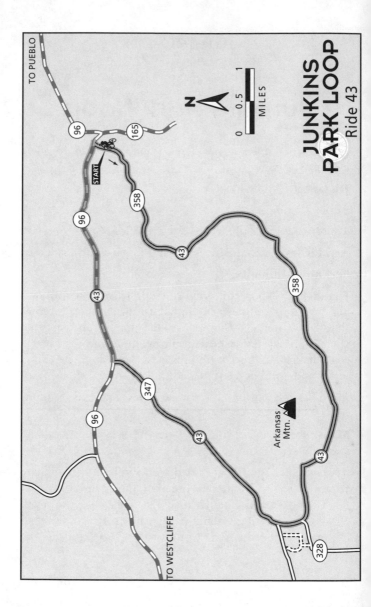

TO PUEBLO

96

165

START

358

96

43

43

347

96

43

Arkansas
Mtn.

358

43

328

TO WESTCLIFFE

N

MILES
0   0.5   1

JUNKINS
PARK LOOP
Ride 43

The Ride

0.0 Head away from CO 96 on County Road 358.
0.9 Cross the cattle guard.
5.3 An elk ranch passes by on the left.
9.1 Leave Junkins Park via a fast and fun descent.
10.1 Turn right, then keep right onto Rosita Road (CR 347).
14.8 Turn right on CO 96. This is the alternate trailhead.
18.8 Back at CR 358.

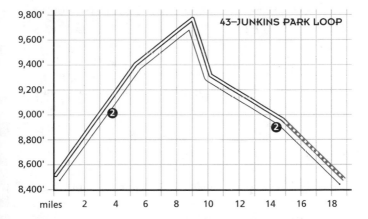

Wet Mountain Valley– Sangre de Cristo Mountains

Westcliffe, 75 miles southwest of Colorado Springs, is the main town in the sparsely populated Wet Mountain Valley. From Colorado Springs drive 35 miles southwest on State Highway 115 through Penrose to Florence. Turn left and take CO 67 11 miles south to Wetmore. Turn right onto CO 96 and drive 27 miles west to Silver Cliff. Westcliffe is 2 miles farther west on CO 96 at the junction with CO 69.

Westcliffe and Silver Cliff offer some quaint lodging along with nearby camping. Groceries and supplies are plentiful, but biking gear is hard to come by. Ask around if you need something. The natives are friendly and will do their best to help out.

The region is ripe with history. Silver Cliff was nearly selected as Colorado's capital when it was a large, influential silver community. More recently, its graveyard was made famous in *National Geographic* for unexplained "ghost lights."

Numerous other settlements once thrived in the area, including a German colony and a group of Spanish conquistadores! The book store in Westcliffe and the museum in Silver Cliff are great places to uncover more information.

44

Ghost Town Loop

Location: 7 miles east of Westcliffe.

Distance: 12.8-mile loop.

Time: 1.5 hours.

Tread: 12.8 miles of dirt road.

Aerobic level: Moderate.

Technical difficulty: 2. A couple of soft shoulders and an occasional car are the main obstacles.

Highlights: Ride through two ghost towns and past numerous old mines. Rosita was a thriving town complete with a brewery, and Querida once boasted a population of 10,000. Old mines, such as the Bassik on Mount Tyndall, produced ore rich in silver and occasionally gold. Keep an eye out for the local elk and deer herds.

Land status: Bureau of Land Management and private holdings.

Maps: San Isabel National Forest; USGS Mount Tyndall, Rosita.

Access: From Westcliffe drive 7.5 miles east on State Highway 96 to County Road 341. Park beside the road.

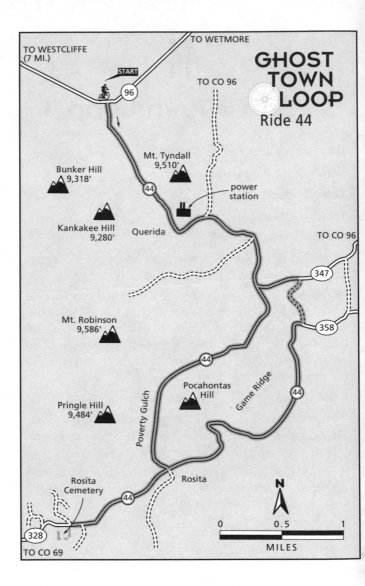

TO WESTCLIFFE
(7 MI.)

TO WETMORE

START

96

TO CO 96

GHOST
TOWN
LOOP
Ride 44

Bunker Hill
9,318'

Mt. Tyndall
9,510'

44

power
station

Kankakee Hill
9,280'

Querida

TO CO 96

347

Mt. Robinson
9,586'

358

44

Pocahontas
Hill

Game Ridge

Poverty Gulch

Pringle Hill
9,484'

44

Rosita
Cemetery

Rosita

N

328

TO CO 69

0   0.5   1

MILES

The Ride

0.0 Ride up County Road 341.

1.3 Welcome to downtown Querida. The chimney on the left is the remains of the old assay office. Mount Tyndall is on the left with the Bassik mine on top.

1.5 Keep right and stay on CR 341. The road to the left is closed to vehicular traffic.

2.4 At the bottom of the hill, turn right onto CR 329.

4.4 Descend through Poverty Gulch into Rosita. Turn right onto CR 328.

5.9 The Rosita Cemetery. Turn around here and retrace your tracks to the junction with CR 329 (see mile 4.4).

7.4 Continue straight on CR 328 and climb along Game Ridge.

9.6 Turn left onto Buttercup Lane.

10.1 Turn left onto CR 347, which soon becomes CR 341.

10.4 Continue straight, retracing the route.

12.8 Back at the car.

Lake DeWeese Loop

Location: 5 miles north of Westcliffe.

Distance: 12.8-mile loop.

Time: 1 hour.

Tread: 8.4 miles of dirt road and 4.4 miles of paved road.

Aerobic level: Moderate. Length will be the main challenge for beginners.

Technical difficulty: 2. Mostly a 2- ride, but the first mile has a couple of 3 spots.

Highlights: Keep company with the Sangre de Cristo Mountains on this level ride as the road loops around DeWeese Reservoir. Abundant waterfowl call this refuge home. The campground here makes a good base of operations when visiting the Wet Mountain Valley. While not a busy road, the traffic on State Highway 69 isn't really expecting bikers so ride accordingly.

Land status: DeWeese Wildlife Refuge and private holdings.

Maps: San Isabel National Forest; USGS Westcliffe.

Access: From Westcliffe drive 0.3 mile north on CO 69. Turn right onto DeWeese Road (County Road 241). Drive east 4.3 miles and take the right fork where the road turns to dirt. Stay on this road past the waste dump station and down to the main parking area. The trail starts at the "modern" outhouses. Water is also available here.

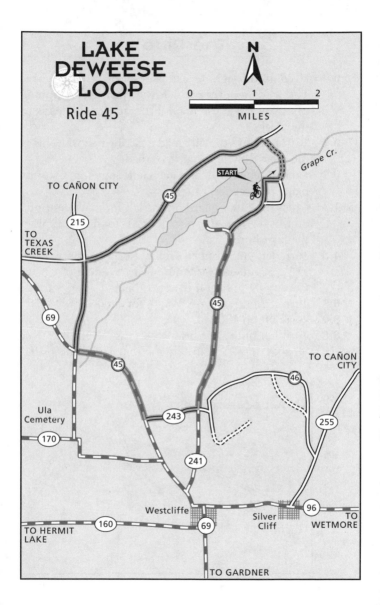

LAKE DEWEESE LOOP

Ride 45

N

0   1   2
MILES

Grape Cr.

START

TO CAÑON CITY

45

215

TO TEXAS CREEK

69

45

45

Ula Cemetery

170

243

241

46

255

TO CAÑON CITY

160

Westcliffe

69

Silver Cliff

96

TO WETMORE

TO HERMIT LAKE

TO GARDNER

The Ride

0.0 Head up through the campsites away from the lake. The roads go every which-way. Just keep climbing until you reach the main dirt road that descends to the creek.

0.2 Turn left onto the dirt road described above. This is the most difficult section of road.

0.5 Cross Grape Creek and keep left. Sometimes storms make this section rough.

1.1 Cross the cattle guard on the left fork and continue on this main road. The side roads to the left explore the lakeshore.

4.8 Turn left on Copper Gulch Road (County Road 215). Scout out St. Andrews at Westcliffe, Custer County's 9-hole golf course.

6.3 Turn left onto CO 69. Watch for cars.

8.0 Turn left on CR 243.

8.8 Turn left onto DeWeese Road (CR 241). The Silver Streak Loop (ride 46) enters from across the road.

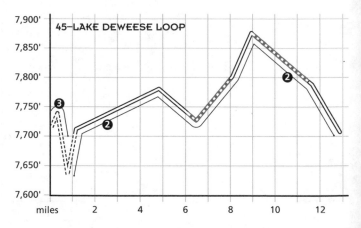

11.5 Take the right fork and follow the dirt road back down to the main parking area.

12.8 Loop's completion.

46

Silver Streak

Location: Westcliffe.

Distance: 6.6-mile loop.

Time: 30 minutes.

Tread: 3.5 miles of dirt road and 3.1 miles of paved road.

Aerobic level: Easy.

Technical difficulty: 2.

Highlights: Fool's gold (iron pyrite) glitters in the sun as you ride through Colorado's silver mining past and among the old pulling shacks and mine tailings that still dot the countryside. Exploring the four-wheel-drive roads in the hills is a great workout aerobically and technically. These optional routes are on the map.

Land status: Bureau of Land Management and private holdings.

Maps: San Isabel National Forest; USGS Westcliffe.

Access: This ride begins in Westcliffe. Parking is available throughout Westcliffe. A good spot is at the Conoco station between Westcliffe and Silver Cliff, or try the school in Westcliffe.

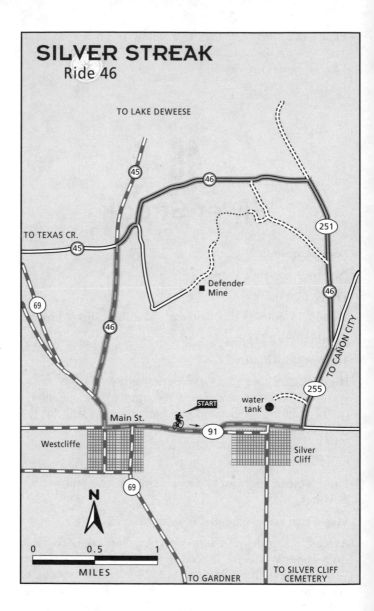

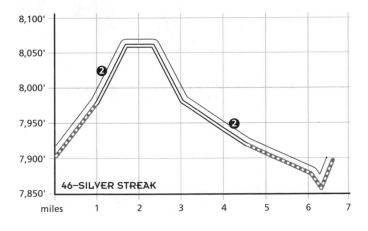

The Ride

0.0 From Westcliffe head up State Highway 96 toward Silver Cliff. The odometer readings start at the Custer County Bank.

1.0 Turn left onto County Road 255. The road descends briefly, crosses a cattle guard, and climbs a short hill.

1.7 Turn left onto CR 251. It is mostly level or downhill from here on out.

2.3 Keep right at this fork. Left is an easy and interesting optional trail.

3.0 Turn left here. Right leads to a trespassing situation.

4.5 Turn right then left onto paved Lake DeWeese Road, which rolls down toward Westcliffe. The optional trail here leads to the Defender mine.

6.0 Turn left onto CO 69 and descend to town.

6.3 Turn left and cruise up Main Street to your car.

6.6 Completion of the loop.

Horn Creek Loop

Location: 8 miles south of Westcliffe.

Distance: 15.9-mile loop.

Time: 2 hours.

Tread: 5.6 miles of singletrack, 5.8 miles of dirt road, and 4.5 miles of paved road.

Aerobic level: Moderate. The majority of the climbing is done on dirt and paved roads.

Technical difficulty: 3+. The singletrack section has some tight spots with a few roots and rocks tossed in.

Highlights: This scenic loop follows a leg of the Rainbow Trail as it contours along the Sangre de Cristo Mountains. The high-lake trails enter the wilderness area and are off-limits to bikes. If using the Alvarado Campground as a base, this makes an excellent first-day ride. To lengthen the loop, simply start pedaling in Westcliffe and follow the directions to the trailhead, where the odometer readings begin.

Land status: San Isabel National Forest and private holdings.

Maps: San Isabel National Forest; USGS Horn Peak.

Access: From Westcliffe drive 3.3 miles south on State Highway 69 to Schoolfield Road (County Road 140) and turn right. Continue straight at the four-way intersection past Macey and Kettle Lanes. At the T intersection turn left

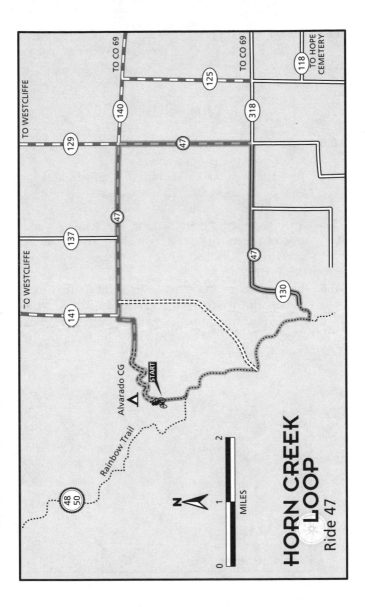

TO WESTCLIFFE

TO WESTCLIFFE

-O WESTCLIFFE

TO CO 69

TO CO 69

129

140

125

137

47

141

47

318

47

130

118

TO HOPE CEMETERY

Alvarado CG

START

Rainbow Trail

48
50

N

MILES

0   1   2

HORN CREEK LOOP

Ride 47

and follow the road up through the Alvarado Campground. The trailhead is at the end of the road. Water is usually available at the trailhead.

The Ride

0.0 Take the well-signed Rainbow Trail access path south from the parking area.

0.5 Turn left onto the Rainbow Trail. The sign here has seen better days! The Hermit Pass route (ride 48) heads off to the right.

5.5 After the thrilling singletrack, the Rainbow Trail crosses the Horn Creek trailhead. Turn left down past Horn Creek Lodge. The trail merges with Horn Road (CR 130).

8.6 Turn left onto Macey Lane (CR 129). In Custer County this passes for a paved road.

10.6 At the four-way junction turn left onto Schoolfield Road (CR 140). The dilapidated building on the right is an old one-room schoolhouse.

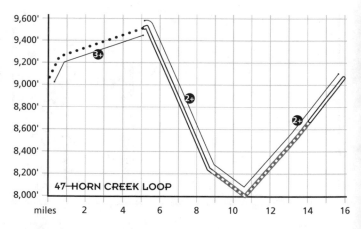

47–HORN CREEK LOOP

13.4 Turn left at the T intersection. This is still CR 140. Stay on this road as it turns to dirt and winds up to Alvarado Campground.

15.9 Back at the trailhead.

Hermit Pass

Location: 8 miles southwest of Westcliffe.

Distance: 21.9 miles out and back.

Time: 5 to 7 hours.

Tread: 9.6 miles of singletrack and 12.3 of rough four-wheel-drive road.

Aerobic level: Strenuous. The singletrack is moderate, but 6.1 miles of extreme climbing on the four-wheel-drive road gives this ride a strenuous rating.

Technical difficulty: 4. The singletrack section rates a 3+, but the continuously rocky four-wheel-drive road justifies the overall rating.

Highlights: The view from above timberline is unforgettable. Add to that four high-country lakes, the Wet Mountain Valley below, a spur to Hermit Lake, beaver ponds, abundant wildlife, and wildflowers galore. It all combines to make this the ultimate trail in the region. When I last rode this loop, snow blocked the final 0.1 or 0.2 mile of the road. This was in August following a heavy-snow winter.

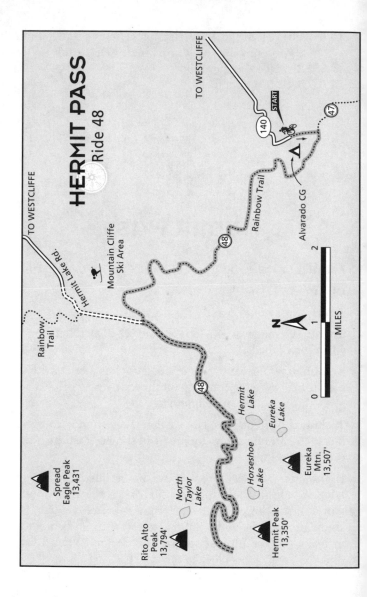

HERMIT PASS
Ride 48

TO WESTCLIFFE

Rainbow Trail

Hermit Lake Rd.

Mountain Cliffe Ski Area

Spread Eagle Peak 13,431'

Rito Alto Peak 13,794'

North Taylor Lake

Hermit Peak 13,350'

Horseshoe Lake

Hermit Lake

Eureka Lake

Eureka Mtn. 13,507'

48

48

Rainbow Trail

48

47

140

START

Alvarado CG

TO WESTCLIFFE

N

MILES

0   1   2

Land status: San Isabel National Forest.

Maps: San Isabel National Forest; USGS Horn Peak.

Access: From Westcliffe drive 3.3 miles south on State Highway 69 to Schoolfield Road (County Road 140) and turn right. Continue straight at the four-way intersection past Macey and Kettle Lanes. At the T intersection turn left and follow the road up through Alvarado Campground. Keep on the campground road all the way to its end (about 0.8 mile), then park. The trail is marked by a large sign and leaves the parking area to the south. There is a water spigot on the northeast side of the parking area.

The Ride

0.0 The first couple hundred yards are actually cemented singletrack. The trail angles south then, and after a couple of switchbacks and a light climb, hits the Rainbow Trail.

0.5 Rainbow Trail. An abused sign marks this trail. Turn right and enjoy the smooth trail. Keep on the Rainbow Trail until it runs into Hermit Lake Road. En route ride past the Comanche, Venable, and

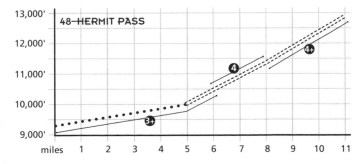

Goodwin trails. The gradual climb on the well-marked Rainbow is occasionally rocky.

4.8 Hermit Lake Road and the Hermit Beaver Ponds. Cross the bridge on the Rainbow Trail and turn left onto the road. Take note of the sign SOME ROADS CLOSED DUE TO . . . This will help you locate the trail on the return trip. Missing the turn means using the valley road system to complete the loop.

8.0 Hermit Lake trailhead. Keep on the road. The trail is a nice sidetrip of about 0.25 mile down to the lake. Then prepare for 3 miles of steep climbs and rocky road to the top of Hermit Pass.

11.0 Top of Hermit Pass. Enjoy the view! Retrace the route for the return trip. The extremely rocky road can be tricky on the downhill. Stop to rest as needed to recover arm strength.

South Colony

Location: 13 miles south of Westcliffe.

Distance: 12.8 miles out and back.

Time: 3 hours.

Tread: 12.8 miles of four-wheel-drive road. The first mile is VERY rough.

Aerobic level: Strenuous. Up, up, up, and more up!

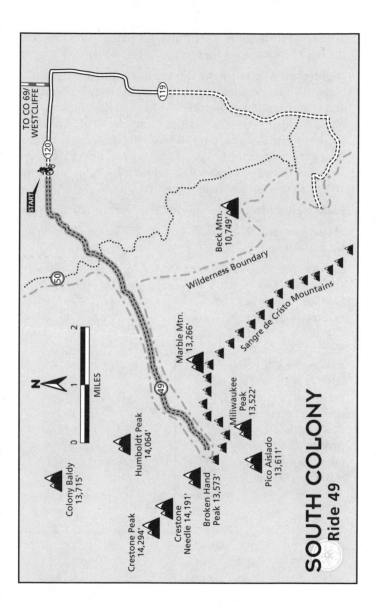

SOUTH COLONY
Ride 49

Technical difficulty: 4. The smooth patches are fine. But the road takes no prisoners when it gets rough!

Highlights: Making it to the top (at 11,300 feet) is the biggest highlight and a true accomplishment. The road's end is surrounded by five 14,000-foot peaks. The Crestone Needle, third from the right, is popular with climbers. Stash the bikes and hike up through the designated wilderness area to South Colony Lakes. Keep an eye on the weather because the bouncy ride down alone can numb the arms and take longer than it seems.

Land status: San Isabel National Forest and private holdings.

Maps: San Isabel National Forest; USGS Crestone Peak, Beck Mountain.

Access: From Westcliffe, drive 4.5 miles south on State Highway 69 to County Road 119 and turn right. Drive another 5.5 miles and turn right onto CR 120. Go up about 1 mile to the parking area. If you have a four-wheel drive you can drive up farther. But don't park on any private land. The odometer readings start at the cattle guard.

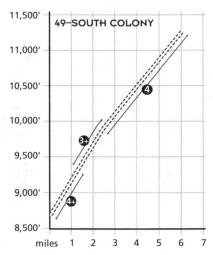

The Ride

0.0 Head up South Colony Road (CR 120).

1.0 The tread becomes noticeably better.

1.8 National Forest boundary.

2.4 Stay on the road as it crosses the Rainbow Trail (see ride 50).

2.8 Cross South Colony Creek.

4.7 Cross the creek again.

6.0 The South Colony Trail passes by on the right. This is one of two ways hikers or equestrians can travel to view the lakes.

6.4 After crossing the creek the trail ends at a gate. Stash your bike here and continue—ON FOOT—straight to see the lakes.

50

Rainbow Trail

Location: West of Westcliffe.

Distance: 32 miles one way.

Time: 5 hours.

Tread: 30.6 miles of singletrack and 1.4 miles of dirt road. This is prime trail!

Aerobic level: Variable. Moderate to strenuous depending on distance and direction ridden.

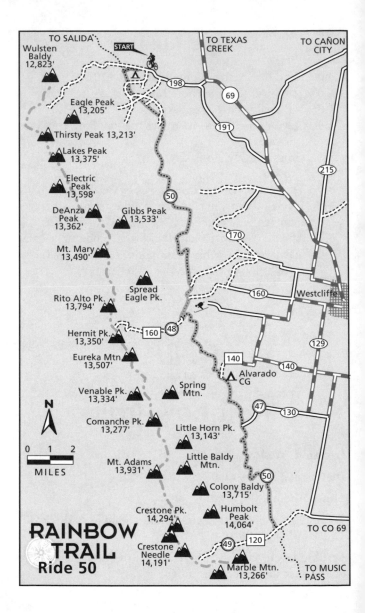

TO SALIDA
START
Wulsten
Baldy
12,823'
TO TEXAS
CREEK
TO CAÑON
CITY
198
69
191
Eagle Peak
13,205'
215
Thirsty Peak 13,213'
Lakes Peak
13,375'
Electric
Peak
13,598'
50
DeAnza
Peak
13,362'
Gibbs Peak
13,533'
170
Mt. Mary
13,490'
160
Spread
Eagle Pk.
Westcliffe
Rito Alto Pk.
13,794'
Hermit Pk.
13,350'
160
48
129
Eureka Mtn
13,507'
140
140
140
Alvarado
CG
Venable Pk.
13,334'
Spring
Mtn.
47
130
Comanche Pk.
13,277'
Little Horn Pk.
13,143'
N
Little Baldy
Mtn.
0   1   2
50
MILES
Mt. Adams
13,931'
Colony Baldy
13,715'
Crestone Pk.
14,294'
Humbolt
Peak
14,064'
TO CO 69
RAINBOW
TRAIL
Ride 50
Crestone
Needle
14,191'
49
120
TO MUSIC
PASS
Marble Mtn.
13,266'

Technical difficulty: 3+. The trail is occasionally narrow and has some rock and root obstacles.

Highlights: The route rolls up and down along the Sangre de Cristo Mountains without much altitude gain. Several access points allow long or short rides and two vehicles makes shuttle rides an option. The views of the Wet Mountain Valley are grand and the up-close look at the mountains is inspirational. Unfortunately the trail has taken tremendous damage from ATVs at a few steep sections. Repairs have been made by an active motorcycle club to help the situation. Let's hope mountain bikers will follow suit and help return this trail to its former glory as one of the best rides in the state.

Land status: San Isabel National Forest and private holdings.

Maps: San Isabel National Forest; USGS Electric Peak, Beckwith Mountain, Horn Peak, Beck Mountain.

Access: Rides 47, 48, and 49 all list possible access points. The ride description given here starts at Lake Creek Campground. From Westcliffe drive 11 miles north on State Highway 69 to County Road 198 and turn left. This dirt road turns toward the mountains and runs into the campground. Incidentally, the road turns into a four-wheel-drive road and leads to Balman Reservoir and Rainbow Lake. Four-wheelers can also access Forest Road 337, FR 332, and FR 331 to get to the trail.

The Ride

- **0.0** The well-signed Rainbow Trail access path leaves the west side of the campground.
- **0.6** Turn left onto the Rainbow Trail proper. Going right the trail runs about 20 miles to Salida!

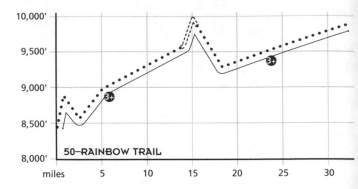

- **1.4** Remain on the trail where it crosses FR 337.
- **2.0** Ditto. Again, remain on the trail across FR 337, followed by FR 332 and FR 338. Stay on the trail throughout.
- **2.4** Keep left and pass by the upper trailhead for Brush Lake.
- **5.3** Keep left and pass by the lower trailhead for Brush Lake.
- **13.0** Turn right on FR 173 and continue up the road. Left leads to Westcliffe.
- **13.4** Turn left onto the Rainbow Trail. Again, it is well signed.
- **14.0** Turn right onto Hermit Lake Road (FR 160). Left here leads to Westcliffe.
- **15.0** Turn left onto the Rainbow Trail. A sign warning SOME ROADS CLOSED DUE TO... marks the turn. Cross the bridge and regain the trail proper.
- **18.3** Keep right as the Alvarado Campground trailhead is down to the left.
- **23.6** Horn Creek access point passes by on the left.
- **32.1** South Colony Road. Turn left to return to Westcliffe or keep riding. The trail ends at Music Pass, but the description stops here.

Appendix A

Additional Ride Information for Colorado Springs

Colorado Springs has a wide variety of city trails available. Palmer Park's terrain offers technical and aerobic challenges. While the city park and recreation department can offer information, the local bike shops remain the best source for these trails. Their fingers are on the pulse of the local fat-tire community.

Garden of the Gods features some fabulous rides amid its world famous rock formations. The Visitor Center offers a map that shows trails and their current status. They've only recently let bikes back onto the trails. Be sure to obey all postings!

The Ring the Peak Trail is getting closer to becoming a reality. This will allow biking around the base of Pikes Peak, looping from Manitou Springs, near the crags, past Cripple Creek, on down near Jones's Downhill, and back over to Manitou Springs.

You may notice some trails missing from this updated edition. The Elk Park–Severy Downhill, Dome Rock, and Cabin Creek Rides have been closed to protect sensitive wildlife areas. However, new areas have been opened up at Mueller State Park and other regions.

The Pikes Peak region is one of the most bike-friendly in the nation. Please keep up the good trail etiquette when looking for new places to ride. Help keep the wheel rolling!

The Manitou Park Bike Trail lies north of Woodland Park on State Highway 67, as do a variety of Forest Service roads. These are accessible at the numerous campgrounds.

Deckers, a small town to the north, has some good trails. Woodland Park bike shops should be able to give you the latest information. The Pike National Forest Map also will help. If you venture into the wilderness areas, go on foot and leave your wheels at the boundary.

Shelf Road and Phantom Canyon are popular dirt-road rides from near Cañon City to Cripple Creek. Jeep roads off Old Stage Road and Gold Camp Road have suitable biking routes. A Pike National Forest map and some USGS topology maps will help you explore these.

The Signal Butte area and Forest Service Trail 717 are good places to expand your wheeled explorations. It's possible to connect to the Rampart Range Road via the 717 series of trails.

Speaking of the Rampart Range Road, a number of four-wheel-drive roads are fun to ride off this gravel highway. Balanced Rock Road connects to Limbaugh Canyon, which connects to the Monument Trail (ride 23) for a ride of epic proportions.

Other local regions also have more trails to offer. Finding out about them is a word-of-mouth matter. Again, the bike shops will be the best bet. A San Isabel Map will help the adventurous find new rides.

The San Carlos Ranger District office is located in Cañon City and has a wealth of information. Get the latest on the region's constantly fluctuating regulations and new trails.

For information on biking in other parts of Colorado, look for Falcon guides to Durango, Boulder, the Aspen-Crested Butte area, the Front Range, and the Fruita/Grand Junction area. Falcon's *Mountain Biking Colorado* is a good starting point for exploring the rest of the state.

Appendix B

Information Sources

USDA Forest Service Offices

Pikes Peak Ranger District–
Pike National Forest
601 S. Weber Street
Colorado Springs, CO 80903
(719) 636–1602

San Carlos Ranger District–San
Isabel National Forest
326 Dozier Avenue
Cañon City, CO 81212
(719) 275–4119

Other Federal Offices

Colorado State BLM Office
2850 Youngfield Street
Lakewood, CO 80215
(303) 239–3600

United States Air Force Academy
2346 Academy Drive
USAF Academy
Colorado Springs, CO
80840-9400
(719) 472–1818

State and Local Agencies

Colorado Division of Wildlife
6060 Broadway
Denver, CO 80216
(303) 297–1192

Colorado Springs Park,
Recreation, and Cultural Services
(719) 385–6540
www.colospgs.com

General Information: (719)
578–6640

Garden Of The Gods Park: (719)
578–6939

Mueller State Park
21045 Highway 67
Divide, CO 80814
(719) 687–2366

Pikes Peak Highway
Superintendent
Cascade, CO 80809
(719) 684–9138
Tollgate: (719) 684–9383

TOPS–Trails, Open Spaces, and
Parks project
(719) 385–6530s

Woodland Park Chamber of
Commerce
P.O. Box 9022
Woodland Park, CO 80866
(719) 687–9885

Glossary

ATB: All-terrain bicycle; a.k.a. mountain bike, sprocket rocket, fat-tire flyer.

ATV: All-terrain vehicle; in this book ATV refers to motorbikes and three- and four-wheelers designed for off-road use.

Bail: Getting off the bike, usually in a hurry, and whether or not you meant to. Often a last resort.

Bunny hop: Leaping up, while riding, and lifting both wheels off the ground to jump over an obstacle (or for sheer joy).

Clean: To ride without touching a foot (or other body part) to the ground; to ride a tough section successfully.

Clipless: A type of pedal with a binding that accepts a matching cleat on the sole of a bike shoe. The cleat locks to the pedal for more control and efficient pedaling, and is easily unlatched for safe landings (in theory).

Contour: A line on a topographic map showing a continuous elevation level over uneven ground. Also a verb indicating a fairly easy or moderate grade: "The trail *contours* around the west flank of the mountain before the final grunt to the top."

Dab: To put a foot or hand down (or hold onto or lean on a tree or other support) while riding. If you have to dab, then you haven't ridden that piece of trail **clean**.

Downfall: Trees that have fallen across the trail.

Doubletrack: A trail, Jeep road, ATV route, or other track with two distinct ribbons of tread, typically with grass growing in between. No matter which side you choose, the other rut always looks smoother.

Endo: Lifting the rear wheel off the ground and riding (or abruptly not riding) on the front wheel only. Also known, at varying degrees of control and finality, as a nose wheelie, going over the handlebars, and a face plant.

Fall line: The line you follow when gravity is in control and you aren't.

Graded: When a gravel road is scraped level to smooth out the washboards and potholes, it has been graded. In this book, a road is listed as graded only if it is regularly maintained. Even these roads are not always graded every year.

Granny gear: The innermost and smallest of the chain rings on the bottom bracket spindle (where the pedals and crank arms attach to the bike's frame). Shift down to your granny gear (and up to the biggest cog on the rear hub) to find your lowest ratio for easiest climbing.

Hammer: To ride hard; derived from how it feels afterward: "I'm hammered."

Hammerhead: Someone who actually enjoys feeling **hammered**. A Type A rider who goes hard and fast all the time.

Line: The route (or trajectory) between or over obstacles or through turns.

Tread or trail refers to the ground you're riding on; the line is the path you choose within the tread (and exists mostly in the eye of the beholder).

Off-the-seat: Moving your butt behind the bike seat and over the rear tire; used for control on extremely steep descents. This position increases braking power, helps prevent endos, and reduces skidding.

Portage: To carry the bike, usually up a steep hill, across unridable obstacles, or through a stream.

Quads: Thigh muscles (short for quadriceps); or maps in the USGS topographic series (short for quadrangles). The right quads (of either kind) can prevent or get you out of trouble in the backcountry.

Ratcheting: Also known as backpedaling; pedaling backward to avoid bashing feet or pedals on rocks or other obstacles.

Sidehill: Where the trail crosses a slope's **fall line**. If the **tread** is narrow, keep your uphill pedal up to avoid hitting the ground. If the tread has a sideways slant, you may have to use body English to keep the bike vertical and avoid side-slipping.

Singletrack: A trail, game run, or other track with only one ribbon of **tread**. But this is like defining an orgasm as a muscle cramp. Good singletrack is pure fun.

Spur: A side road or trail that splits off from the main route.

Surf: Riding through loose gravel or sand, when the wheels slalom from side to side. Also *heavy surf:* frequent and difficult obstacles.

Suspension: A bike with front suspension has a shock-absorbing fork or stem. Rear suspension absorbs shock between the rear wheel and frame. A bike with both is said to be fully suspended.

Switchbacks: When a trail goes up a steep slope, it zigzags or switchbacks across the **fall line** to ease the gradient of the climb. Well-designed switchbacks make a turn with at least an 8-foot radius and remain fairly level within the turn itself. These are rare, however, and cyclists often struggle to ride through sharply angled, sloping switchbacks.

Track stand: Balancing on a bike in one place, without rolling forward appreciably. Cock the front wheel to one side and bring that pedal up to the 1 or 2 o'clock position. Now control your side-to-side balance by applying pressure on the pedals and brakes and changing the angle of the front wheel, as needed. It takes practice but really comes in handy at stoplights, on **switchbacks**, and when trying to free a foot before falling (see **clipless**).

Tread: The riding surface, particularly regarding **singletrack**.

Water bar: A log, rock, conveyor belting, ditch, or other barrier placed in the **tread** to divert water off the trail and prevent erosion. Peeled logs can be slippery and cause bad falls, especially when they angle sharply across the trail.

Whoop-te-doo: An abrupt mound of dirt across the road or trail. These are common on old logging roads and skidder tracks, placed there to block vehicle access. At high speeds, they become launching pads that transform bikes into spaceships and riders into astronauts.

A Short Index of Rides

Road Rides
(may include Jeep tracks and unmaintained routes)

Sweet Singletrack Rides
(may also include road and doubletrack portions)

Beginner's Luck

Technical Tests

Great Climbs—the Yearn to Burn

Great Downhills—the Need for Speed

About the Author

Hmm...what do you want to know about me?

I've loved the outdoors for as long as I can remember. I hiked, fished, spelunked, and rode while growing up in the Wet Mountain Valley.

Mountain biking as such didn't exist back then. We'd con a parent into shuttling our BMX bikes up to Alvarado Campground (see ride 47) and then ride around and bomb back to Westcliffe. I inherited a ten-speed from my brother and began riding around the old mining roads (see rides 44, 45, and 46). That poor bike!

Biking took a backseat while I went to Colorado State University and still hadn't resurfaced during my "professional" career. In Summit County, Colorado, while ski-bumming, my biking passion was rekindled.

Anyway, that's my mountain-biking background.

Professionally I wear many hats. Photographer and writer are the most recent. I've been a private investigator, counseled behaviorally disturbed adolescents, and been a salesman for a variety of things. My official education got me a Bachelor of Science degree in Psychology.

I am currently on hiatus, taking a break from Colorado. I've lived in the state since 1976 and treasure it! But I need something to compare it to. As we go to press, I'm learning to surf in California.

I guess the main thing to know about me is that I enjoy life.

I hope this guide increases your enjoyment.

UPDATE: Since penning this book, I've written *Mountain Biking Moab, Exploring Southern California Beaches,* and am currently working on *Exploring Capitol Reef National Park* . . .

More importantly, I got married in 2000. My wife, Heidi, a wildlife biologist, opens my eyes daily to new ways to absorb the goodness that is life.

My son, Dawson, was born as we went to press. This new leg of my journey has my soul overflowing with happiness.

I hope my guidebooks help you on you on your own journey.

Enjoy!
Dave